TOUR DE FARCE:
A New Series of Farce Through the Ages

A SLAP IN THE FARCE

(LA MAIN LESTE)

& A MATTER OF
WIFE AND DEATH

(LA LETTRE CHARGÉE)

by Eugène Labiche

Adapted and Translated
by Norman R. Shapiro

APPLAUSE
THEATRE BOOK PUBLISHERS
211 West 71 Street, New York, NY 10023

Library of Congress Cataloging in Publication Data

Labiche, Eugène, 1815-1888.
   [Main leste. English]
   A slap in the farce ; & A matter of wife and death / by Eugène Labiche ; adapted and translated by Norman R. Shapiro.
      p. cm.\— (Tour de farce)
   Translation of : La Main leste ; and La Lettre chargée.
   Original titles appear as parallel titles on t.p.
   ISBN 0-936839-82-1 : $7.95
   1. Labiche, Eugène, 1815-1888—Translations, English.
I. Shapiro, Norman R. II. Labiche, Eugène, 1815-1888. Lettre chargée. English. III. Title. IV. Title: Slap in the farce. V. Title: Matter of wife and death. VI. Series.
PQ2321.A27 1988
842'.8—dc19
                                    88-22178
                                       CIP

APPLAUSE THEATRE BOOK PUBLISHERS
211 W. 71st Street, New York, NY 10023
(212) 595-4735

First Applause Printing, 1988

CONTENTS

A SLAP IN THE FARCE

(LA MAIN LESTE)

by

Eugène Labiche and Édouard Martin

(1867)

Characters:

ANTOINE
LECOUQUE
MADAME LECOUQUE
CÉLINE
MADAME DE RIGUEUR

Scene:

The dining room in the Lecouque household. Upstage center, a double door leading onto a vestibule. Down right and down left, two more doors. Left, a dining table and three chairs. On the table, cups and saucers, a pitcher of coffee, and the remains of lunch. Against the upstage wall, far right, a set of shelves covered with ladies' flowered hats. Close to it, by the wall, right, a work table with assorted articles: artificial flowers, ribbons, several finished hats, and a small bell. Against the upstage wall, far left, a cupboard for dishware, etc. On it, a bowl of fruit. Near the door, down right, a small desk and chair, facing the audience, with paper, inkwell and pen. Midstage, right of center, a small loveseat. Next to it, an end table. Other appropriate furnishings—occasional chairs, pictures, etc.—ad lib.

At rise, LECOUQUE, MADAME LECOUQUE *and* CÉLINE *are seated around the table, left, finishing their lunch.*

MADAME LECOUQUE *(to* LECOUQUE, *impatiently)*: Well? Are you going to take all day?

LECOUQUE: My love?

MADAME LECOUQUE: With your coffee! I've never seen anyone take so long...

LECOUQUE: But it's too hot... Look...

(He holds up the steaming cup.)

MADAME LECOUQUE: And whose fault is that? You always want it boiling! Not one degree less!

LECOUQUE: Of course... So it can cool... *(Placing the cup under his nose.)* I love the aroma...

MADAME LECOUQUE: If you think it's a pleasure watching you sniff at it for an hour...

LECOUQUE: A real connoisseur, my love, drinks coffee twice... First with the nose, and then—

MADAME LECOUQUE *(interrupting)*: Connoisseur, my foot! You're absolutely impossible!

LECOUQUE: Temper, temper, temper! *(Getting up and offering her the fruit basket on the cupboard, up left.)* Here, have a banana... It will help pass the time.

MADAME LECOUQUE: I don't want a banana! Lunch is over! I've finished!

(She stands up and begins pacing back and forth.)

LECOUQUE *(putting back the basket and sitting down again, aside)*: Forward, march! One, two, one, two...

MADAME LECOUQUE *(stopping suddenly, looking at* CÉLINE): And you!... Oh!

CÉLINE: Me, Mamma? What have I—

MADAME LECOUQUE: Sitting there, staring at your coffee, like a... like a mummy!

CÉLINE: But...

LECOUQUE: Really, Hildegarde...

MADAME LECOUQUE: Like father, like daughter! The two of you are impossible!

CÉLINE: But...

LECOUQUE: I told you...

CÉLINE: I can't very well pour it down Papa's throat, can I? It's too hot!

MADAME LECOUQUE: Hot? Ha!... *(She picks up* LECOUQUE's *coffee and downs it in one gulp.)* There! That's how hot it is!

LECOUQUE: What do you think you're... That's my coffee, for heaven's sake! How many times... *(Getting up.)* If you want some, pour your own!

CÉLINE: Where are you going, Mamma?

MADAME LECOUQUE: To the police station.

LECOUQUE: The police—

MADAME LECOUQUE: Don't worry! Only the Lost and Found...

CÉLINE: Did you lose something?

MADAME LECOUQUE: Yes... Last night, in the tram... I was sitting next to an absolutely insufferable individual... The most impolite...

LECOUQUE *(aside)*: She lost her temper!

MADAME LECOUQUE: The most ill-mannered, insolent...

LECOUQUE *(to* MADAME LECOUQUE*)*: Let me guess... He insulted you...

MADAME LECOUQUE: The most...

LECOUQUE: Well, what did he say?

MADAME LECOUQUE: Can you imagine? He... *(Noticing* CÉLINE, *hanging on her words.)* Céline, darling... I think you'd better go to the shop and make sure those good-for-nothings aren't twiddling their thumbs!

CÉLINE: Yes, Mamma! *(Aside.)* I never get to hear the good parts!

(She exits, right.)

LECOUQUE: Well, what did this insufferable, insolent, ill-mannered young man have to say?

MADAME LECOUQUE: Young man?

LECOUQUE: Yes... I thought you said... Wasn't it a man?

MADAME LECOUQUE: Oh yes! It was a man!... It most certainly was a man!

LECOUQUE: Well?

MADAME LECOUQUE: But young?... Old?... I have no idea... I never saw his face!

LECOUQUE: You what?

MADAME LECOUQUE: No... The kerosene lamps were broken and we were practically in the dark.

LECOUQUE: Of all things...

MADAME LECOUQUE: Well, all of a sudden I felt him bending over and reaching down, and... and... You'll never believe the gall...

LECOUQUE: And...?

MADAME LECOUQUE: And he put his hand on my shoes! You know... The fancy ones... With the fur...

LECOUQUE: No! *(Aside.)* It takes all kinds!

MADAME LECOUQUE: Then he began to stroke my foot. And he kept whispering: "Pretty baby, pretty baby!"

LECOUQUE *(aside)*: Dark? It must have been pitch black!

MADAME LECOUQUE *(almost overhearing)*: What?

LECOUQUE: Nothing, my love... Nothing... Please... Please, go on...

MADAME LECOUQUE: Well, you can just imagine!... I was absolutely furious! The nerve of some people!... I mean...

LECOUQUE: Don't tell me... Let me guess... You slapped him!

MADAME LECOUQUE: I certainly did! Wouldn't you?

LECOUQUE *(musing)*: If he stroked my foot?... Yes, I suppose...

MADAME LECOUQUE: Right in the face... A good one, too... And he felt it, I can tell you!

LECOUQUE: I'm sure!

MADAME LECOUQUE: He went: "Ayyy!... My eye! My eye!..."

LECOUQUE *(aside)*: Ayyy! Ayyy! Ayyy!

MADAME LECOUQUE: Well, I got up and told the conductor to stop right there! And I got off in a huff! I wasn't going to stay on that tram another minute!

LECOUQUE: I hope he refunded half your fare at least...

MADAME LECOUQUE: My fare? That was the least of my worries, believe me?

LECOUQUE: After all, six sous...

MADAME LECOUQUE: Unfortunately, I hadn't taken more than a couple of steps, when I realized that my handbag was still on my seat... With my purse inside... Full of money...

LECOUQUE: No!

MADAME LECOUQUE: Yes!... Forty-six francs, twenty-five centimes...

LECOUQUE: Damn!

MADAME LECOUQUE: I'm just hoping that somebody found it... Somebody honest, that is... Not that... that sex fiend!

LECOUQUE: Now, now, Hildegarde... Some sex fiends might be honest...

MADAME LECOUQUE: Well... That's why I'm going to the police station... Maybe somebody turned it in. *(Examining her attire for a moment.)* Hmm... I'd better put on something fancy, don't you think? They're much more polite when you come in with lots of frills...

LECOUQUE *(aside)*: I never noticed.

MADAME LECOUQUE: ...and when you're pretty...

LECOUQUE: Yes, my love... *(Aside.)* Go do your best!

MADAME LECOUQUE *(overhearing)*: I beg your pardon?

LECOUQUE: "Oh, do get dressed!" I said... "Do get dressed!"... Of course, not that you need to... *(Slyly.)* You pretty baby!

MADAME LECOUQUE: Oh... Be quiet, you...

(She exits, left.)

LECOUQUE: Poor Hildegarde! For once she's right, and it costs her forty-six francs... And twenty-five centimes!... And all because some maniac falls in love with her foot!... Well, I've got other things to worry about too... Duty calls! *(He gets up, goes over to the work table, right, and picks up a hat, holding it up, admiringly.)* Ah! My latest creation!... Another stunning Lecouque original!... Next week my competitors will be green with envy!... I call it "Widow's Weeds"... *(Fondling the flowers.)* Even though they're violets... Nice dark ones, of course... For widows, after all... Dark enough to be decent, but not quite enough to... *(Knowingly.)* discourage admirers!... It's bound to be all the rage... Perfect for widows with serious intentions...

(The double door opens and MADAME DE RIGUEUR *strides in.)*

MADAME DE RIGUEUR: Ah, monsieur! There you are!

LECOUQUE: Madame de Rigueur!... *(Aside.)* Speak of the devil! *(Aloud.)* And what can I do for my favorite customer? *(Aside.)* And one of the richest!

MADAME DE RIGUEUR: I'm looking for something very special, monsieur.

LECOUQUE: A hat?

MADAME DE RIGUEUR: Of course... But something utterly chic...

LECOUQUE: For a ball?

MADAME DE RIGUEUR: No...

LECOUQUE: A dinner?

MADAME DE RIGUEUR: No...

LECOUQUE: The theater?

MADAME DE RIGUEUR: No, no... It's rather hard to explain... Some friends are coming over this afternoon... The baroness, the countess... And some gentlemen... Writers... We're going to read poetry. It's all terribly intellectual.

LECOUQUE: Yes... I see... A literary soirée, you might say... Only in the afternoon...

MADAME DE RIGUEUR: Yes... Quite...

LECOUQUE: Well, madame, I have exactly what you're looking for! A new creation... My latest... In fact, it's so new, I'm not showing it until next week. But for you, madame... And it's perfect for widows, if you don't mind my saying... *(He shows her the hat.)* See? An inspiration, if I do say so myself!

MADAME DE RIGUEUR *(sitting on the loveseat and examining the hat)*: Don't you find it a... a trifle plain?

LECOUQUE: Plain?

MADAME DE RIGUEUR: Yes... Rather undistinguished...

LECOUQUE *(taken aback)*: Well, I don't think...

MADAME DE RIGUEUR: What kind of flowers are these, monsieur?

LECOUQUE: Violets... Violets, madame... Dark ones, of course... Dark enough to be decent, but not quite enough to—

MADAME DE RIGUEUR: No... No, thank you... No violets... They're much too banal!... Common... Common...

LECOUQUE *(putting the hat back on the work table)*: Well... It's a matter of opinion...

MADAME DE RIGUEUR: No... I had in mind something rather more... poetic.

LECOUQUE: Yes... Yes, of course...

MADAME DE RIGUEUR: Vaguely expressive, but... but tender and... subdued...

LECOUQUE *(nodding)*: Aha...

MADAME DE RIGUEUR: Something that... that sings...

LECOUQUE *(aside)*: Sings?

MADAME DE RIGUEUR: Striking, but... utterly unobtrusive!... You do see what I mean, monsieur?

LECOUQUE: Oh... Perfectly!... Perfectly!

MADAME DE RIGUEUR: I was sure you would.

LECOUQUE: Perhaps a simple tiara... Tea roses, madame... With just a touch of fern... They're very poetic, and... they sing, madame... They sing...

MADAME DE RIGUEUR *(rather disdainfully)*: Tea roses?

LECOUQUE: Well, dark ones... I mean, considering... Pearl grey... Or a nice navy blue...

MADAME DE RIGUEUR: Blue?... I didn't think tea roses came in navy blue.

LECOUQUE: No... Not in the wild, as they say... But in society... In the very best salons...

MADAME DE RIGUEUR: Oh?

LECOUQUE: Yes, they're terribly chic... *(Trying to recall her words.)* Vaguely expressive, but... but tender...

MADAME DE RIGUEUR: And subdued?

LECOUQUE: Oh yes! Yes... Very...

MADAME DE RIGUEUR: Well, perhaps... Can you show me, monsieur?

LECOUQUE: Certainly! *(With a grandiose gesture toward the door, down right.)* If you'll just step into the shop, madame... I'm sure Mademoiselle Céline will be only too delighted...

MADAME DE RIGUEUR *(getting up, musing)*: Navy blue tea roses... Yes, they might sing... They might...

LECOUQUE: Oh, they do, madame!... They do! But ever so discreetly... *(As MADAME DE RIGUEUR reaches the door, nodding.)* Madame...

MADAME DE RIGUEUR: Monsieur...

(She exits.)

LECOUQUE *(moving left)*; Charming lady... Charming!... A little... *(He shrugs.)* But charming!

(ANTOINE appears at the double door, up center. His hair is combed over one eye, and he is carrying a lady's handbag.)

ANTOINE *(entering)*: Excuse me... Madame Lecouque?

LECOUQUE: Madame...? Do I look like Madame Lecouque?

ANTOINE: No, no, monsieur... I mean... Does she live here?

LECOUQUE: Of course she does! She's my wife!

ANTOINE: Ah!... Then she must be married...

LECOUQUE: One would think so!

ANTOINE: Good! That makes things so much easier, monsieur.

LECOUQUE: It does?

ANTOINE: Oh, much!

LECOUQUE: Easier than what?

ANTOINE: I'll explain in a moment, monsieur... All in due time...

(There is an awkward silence as both men eye each other.)

LECOUQUE: Well?

ANTOINE: I'm returning this handbag...

LECOUQUE: You're returning... Oh my! Why didn't you say... You mean, the one Hildegarde... the one Madame Lecouque left in the tram last night?

ANTOINE: Precisely, monsieur... I took the liberty of opening it... To look inside, you understand...

LECOUQUE: Of course...

ANTOINE: I couldn't do one without the other...

LECOUQUE: No, no... Quite all right...

ANTOINE: And I found your name and address, monsieur... That is, madame's...

LECOUQUE: Yes... yes...

ANTOINE: And forty-six francs, twenty-five centimes... It's all there... Down to the last centime...

(He gives LECOUQUE *the handbag.)*

LECOUQUE: I don't doubt it, monsieur... I'm... We're terribly grateful, madame and I... *(Aside.)* I won't insult him by offering him a reward... Just a few well-chosen words of appreciation... *(Aloud.)* It's all too rare, in this day and age, monsieur, to find someone so honest... so considerate... You're a gentleman! My congratulations!

ANTOINE: Thank you... And now that that's taken care of, we can talk about another little problem, monsieur.

LECOUQUE: We can?

ANTOINE: If I may...

LECOUQUE: Yes... Please, I insist!... What kind of problem?

ANTOINE: An affront to my honor, monsieur! Madame Lecouque, if you don't mind my saying, is rather free with her hand!

LECOUQUE *(surprised)*: What?... You mean, you're the one... the man... the one she...

ANTOINE: Yes, monsieur. In the eye... As I think you can see...

(He brushes back his hair, revealing a black eye.)

LECOUQUE *(examining it)*: My, my... Yes, I... Yes, indeed...

ANTOINE: I think I've proved my point, monsieur.

LECOUQUE: Yes, I would say... But you have to admit, you did have it coming!

ANTOINE: I did?

LECOUQUE: After all, you asked for it...

ANTOINE: Excuse me, monsieur, but... Your meaning eludes me...

LECOUQUE: Well, really!... Gentlemen don't go around stroking strange ladies' feet... Unless they get their permission, that is...

ANTOINE: Strange ladies' what?

LECOUQUE: Of course! Play dumb!... I suppose you deny it!

ANTOINE: "It," monsieur?

LECOUQUE: Stroking my wife's foot last night?

ANTOINE *(dumbfounded)*: What?

LECOUQUE: In the tram!

ANTOINE *(self-righteously)*: I beg your pardon!... I never...

LECOUQUE: Then why did you bend down? Why were you whispering sweet nothings, if I may ask...

ANTOINE *(speechless)*: Sweet... Monsieur, I was stroking my dog!... My pekingese... My little Chin-Chin...

LECOUQUE: Your...

ANTOINE: She was under the seat, but she wouldn't keep still. So, naturally, I bent down and tried to... You know... *(He bends down, as if patting a dog.)* "Pretty baby... Pretty baby..."

LECOUQUE: Oh my... My, my... And my wife... With her fancy shoes... The ones with the fur... She thought... She thought... *(Chuckling.)* "Pretty baby!"

(He bursts out laughing.)

ANTOINE: I'm glad you find it amusing, monsieur.

LECOUQUE: Amusing?... *(Still laughing.)* It's hilarious!... Hildegarde... You thought... *(After a pause.)* Why aren't you laughing?

ANTOINE: I'm afraid I'm not amused.

LECOUQUE: Oh?

ANTOINE: You're forgetting... *(Pointing to his eye.)* My honor...

LECOUQUE: Come, come now, my friend!... You don't mean to tell me... An innocent little slap... And from a pretty lady...

ANTOINE: Pretty, monsieur?

LECOUQUE: Well... "Ish..."

ANTOINE: I beg your pardon?

LECOUQUE: Prettyish... Prettyish...

ANTOINE: Aha...

LECOUQUE: And, after all, she thought... I mean, it was all a mistake... Besides, she slaps me all the time, but do I make a fuss?

ANTOINE: She does?

LECOUQUE: Well, once in a while... She tends to be rather free with her hands!

ANTOINE: Yes, well... You, monsieur, are her husband. You have to expect it... And I assume you slap her back?

LECOUQUE: Her back?... *(Comprehending.)* Oh, "slap her back..." No, no, monsieur! Certainly not!... I kiss her!

ANTOINE: You do?

LECOUQUE: Of course!... *(Gallantly.)* A lady's slap deserves a kiss in return! Don't you agree?... She's free with her hands... I'm free with my lips!

ANTOINE *(nodding)*: I see... I see...

LECOUQUE *(ready to end the conversation)*: Well then...

ANTOINE: Yes, monsieur... That's quite acceptable.

LECOUQUE: Please?

ANTOINE: That will be fine with me.

LECOUQUE: What will be fine with you?

ANTOINE: I'm willing to kiss your wife, monsieur.

LECOUQUE *(with a start)*: You're willing to...

(He laughs incredulously.)

ANTOINE: As a favor, of course...

LECOUQUE: Who said anything about—

ANTOINE: Please don't misunderstand. It's not that I have any... well, lubricious designs... I've never had the pleasure of meeting Madame Lecouque... Not face to face...

LECOUQUE: No, not quite!

ANTOINE: Last night doesn't count... Her foot, I mean...

LECOUQUE: Yes...

ANTOINE: It's just that it seems like an honorable way to... how shall I say?... to resolve our affair.

LECOUQUE *(moving upstage)*: Oh? Kiss my wife? Honorable?... I hardly think so!

ANTOINE: But, monsieur...

LECOUQUE: Never!... Certainly not!

ANTOINE *(crossing left)*: Then I'm afraid I have no choice... I'll have to challenge you to a duel, monsieur.

LECOUQUE: Me?... Why me, for heaven's sake?

ANTOINE: Well, really! I can't very well run a sword through your wife! You wouldn't want that, I'm sure! Whereas, with you... Well...

LECOUQUE: What?

ANTOINE: I mean, you *are* her husband! The law says you're responsible...

LECOUQUE: But...

ANTOINE: And a slap, monsieur... In the face... I don't have to tell you... Besides, in front of everybody... Dozens of people...

LECOUQUE: So what? A pack of strangers... And it was dark!

ANTOINE: Not dark enough!... And they weren't all strangers either! A gentleman of my acquaintance was seated next to me, monsieur!

LECOUQUE: Oh?

ANTOINE: An associate... One of my Aix colleagues...

LECOUQUE: What difference does it make? You'll probably never see him.

ANTOINE: On the contrary, monsieur... I see him every day! I'll be the laughingstock... All our friends will know...

LECOUQUE: But... You said "ex-colleague"... I thought...

ANTOINE: Aix, monsieur... Aix-en-Provence... Near Marseille...

LECOUQUE: Oh...

ANTOINE: That's where we learned to paint... The two of us...

LECOUQUE: Paint, monsieur?... You're a painter?

ANTOINE: I daresay...

LECOUQUE: Houses?

ANTOINE: No, no... Portraits, mainly... At least, that's what everyone says I do best... *(As* LECOUQUE, *happy to change the subject, nods knowingly.)* They're really quite out of the ordinary...

LECOUQUE: I'm sure...

ANTOINE: If you know anyone who would like one done, they're forty francs...

LECOUQUE *(nodding)*: Forty...

ANTOINE: In oils, of course...

LECOUQUE: Of course...

ANTOINE: Not exactly a fortune...

LECOUQUE: No... I should say...

ANTOINE *(after a pause, abruptly)*: Well, have you decided?

LECOUQUE: On a portrait?

ANTOINE: No, no... First things first... Do I kiss your wife, or do I kill you, monsieur? It's one or the other.

LECOUQUE: But... Just like that? Kiss my... You have to admit, it's not every day... "May I kiss your wife, monsieur?"... Really, you have to admit...

ANTOINE *(dryly)*: I admit, monsieur... Now what have you decided?

LECOUQUE *(relenting)*: Well, I suppose... That is, if she doesn't mind... I mean, what's the harm, as long as you don't enjoy it...

ANTOINE: Oh, I wouldn't, monsieur... I wouldn't...

LECOUQUE: And as long as I'm watching... You understand...

ANTOINE: Quite all right... You won't disturb me.

LECOUQUE: Of course, I will have to discuss the matter first with Madame Lecouque.

ANTOINE: Certainly! I think that's only proper.

LECOUQUE: If you'll give me a few minutes... *(Indicating the loveseat.)* Please, make yourself comfortable... I won't be very long... *(Aside, leaving.)* Good God! She'll never... He strokes her foot and I ask her to kiss him!... Never!... Never in a million years...

(He exits, left.)

ANTOINE *(sitting down on the loveseat)*: Well, it's not exactly what I had in mind, but... All things considered... I'd say I've handled the affair rather nicely!... A kiss for a slap! What could be more gallant?... And a pretty young thing... Hot-tempered, passionate... They'll love it at the club... I can just see their faces!... Tonight, at dinner... Over a glass of Saint-Émilion... Three francs a bottle... "You mean, you kissed her?... Yes, that's what I said! I kissed her!..." What panache!... *(Looking at his watch.)* Hmm! I wonder what's keeping her... You don't suppose she said no...

(CÉLINE enters, right, without noticing ANTOINE, and keeps crossing left.)

CÉLINE *(suddenly noticing him, aside)*: Oh my! A man...

ANTOINE *(getting up, aside)*: Well, well, well! I must say, she's worth waiting for! *(To CÉLINE, bowing.)* Madame...

CÉLINE *(aside)*: Who is he, I wonder?

ANTOINE *(rather pompously)*: Permit me to say how grateful I am to be the victim... the happy victim... of a momentary lapse...

CÉLINE *(aside)*: A customer, I imagine...

ANTOINE: No hard feelings, madame... I assure you, no hard feelings... *(Gallantly.)* Especially since the remedy will amply repair any minor discomfort...

CÉLINE *(puzzled)*: Monsieur?

ANTOINE: Oh, more than amply!... Trams can be such a nuisance, but I'm really not sorry!

CÉLINE *(aside)*: He came by tram?

ANTOINE *(aside)*: Poor thing! She's so embarrassed! *(Aloud.)* Come now... A stiff upper lip... So to speak!... It won't take long...

CÉLINE: Monsieur?

ANTOINE: Are you ready?

CÉLINE: Ready? For what?

ANTOINE: To make amends, madame. After all, there's nothing that can't be mended, if we put our minds to it! *(Aside.)* Even honor!

CÉLINE *(moving to the work table)*: Oh! You had something to be mended, monsieur? *(Aside.)* Why didn't he say so?

ANTOINE: Indeed, madame! That's one way of putting it...

CÉLINE *(picking up one of the hats)*: This one must be yours, monsieur. It was brought in yesterday to have the lilac sewn back on...

ANTOINE: Mine?... That?... I hardly think so... Besides, madame, I seldom wear a hat... *(Looking askance at the hat.)* Any kind of hat... Even when I'm painting...

CÉLINE *(replacing the hat)*: Painting, monsieur?

ANTOINE: Yes, madame... Portraits, mainly... If you know anyone who would like one done... Forty francs... In oils, of course...

CÉLINE *(nodding)*: I see... I see... *(After an embarrassed pause.)* Then... What was it you had in mind, monsieur?

ANTOINE: What was it I... You mean, he didn't tell you?

CÉLINE: Who, monsieur? Tell me what?

ANTOINE: Your... Monsieur Lecouque... Didn't he...

CÉLINE: Papa?

ANTOINE *(taken back)*: Papa?

CÉLINE: What did Papa have to tell me, monsieur?

ANTOINE: Papa?... Papa?... *(Aside.)* Good God! It's his daughter! *(Aloud.)* Madame... Mademoiselle... He's your daughter... I mean, you're his... He's your father...

CÉLINE: Papa?... Of course, monsieur!

ANTOINE *(bumbling)*: And you... you have a mother?

CÉLINE: Why, yes...

ANTOINE: And she wears shoes?

CÉLINE: Monsieur?

ANTOINE: Fancy ones... With fur?

CÉLINE: Yes, sometimes... When it's cold...

ANTOINE *(aside)*: Damn! It's her mother!... She's no chicken, that's for sure! *(Aloud.)* Excuse me, mademoiselle, but... May I ask how old you are?

CÉLINE: Why, I'm eighteen, monsieur... But I really don't see—

ANTOINE: And your mother... How old was she when she married your father?

CÉLINE: I beg your pardon?

ANTOINE *(musing)*: Let's say eighteen, more or less... So... Eighteen and eighteen... Thirty-six, give or take... *(Aside.)* No!... No chicken!... *(Aloud.)* Tell me, does she still have her hair?

CÉLINE: Monsieur?

ANTOINE: I mean, all the same color?... All still blonde?

CÉLINE: Brown, monsieur... But—

ANTOINE: Yes, yes... Whatever... But not grey?

CÉLINE: Really, I don't... *(Suddenly.)* Oh, I know, monsieur!... I know why you're here!... You're a painter, and you're going to paint her portrait! Of course!

ANTOINE: Well... Not quite, mademoiselle... I'm here on a rather emotional mission...

CÉLINE: Emotional, monsieur?

ANTOINE: And terribly delicate...

CÉLINE: A delicate mission... *(Aside.)* Oh my! He must be... Of course! He's a suitor! Papa didn't tell me...

ANTOINE: I'm afraid I'd better not go into detail, but... Well, just let me say, mademoiselle, that... that I certainly hope you look like your mother!

CÉLINE: You do?

ANTOINE: Oh yes!... Fervently!

CÉLINE: My goodness, monsieur... Why?

ANTOINE: Because then she would look like you, and... and...

CÉLINE: Yes?

ANTOINE: And... Well, it's just that... It would make things so much easier, mademoiselle...

CÉLINE: Monsieur?

ANTOINE: In the tram, I mean...

CÉLINE: In the... *(Aside.)* He's so nervous, poor thing!... He doesn't know what he's saying!

ANTOINE: My Chin-Chin... My little Chin-Chin... It was dark and... The shoes...

CÉLINE *(aside)*: Good heavens! He's babbling!

ANTOINE: No, no... I really can't go into detail... I... It's... Just believe me when I tell you that... that the more I look at you like this... the more... the more I have a feeling...

CÉLINE: A feeling, monsieur?

ANTOINE *(abruptly)*: Could you possibly be persuaded, mademoiselle... That is, if your mother had a... a debt... Would you be willing to pay it?

CÉLINE: A debt? Mamma?

ANTOINE: So to speak...

CÉLINE: What kind? What do I have to do?

ANTOINE: Nothing, really... You just have to stand there and... *(Approaching her.)* and let me do the rest...

(He takes her hand.)

CÉLINE *(startled)*: Monsieur!

ANTOINE: Just pretend I have a secret... *(Bending toward her.)* to whisper in your ear...

(MADAME DE RIGUEUR enters, right.)

MADAME DE RIGUEUR *(speaking over her shoulder, into the wings)*: Today!... You won't forget!

ANTOINE *(just as he is about to kiss CÉLINE on the cheek)*: Damn! Too late!

MADAME DE RIGUEUR: Because if not... Well... *(To CÉLINE, suddenly noticing her.)* You will see to it my child... Today?

ANTOINE *(aside)*: "My..." Her child?

CÉLINE *(to MADAME DE RIGUEUR)*: Yes, of course...

ANTOINE *(aside)*: That's her mother?... *(Looking MADAME DE RIGUEUR up and down, still aside.)* Hmm! Not bad...

MADAME DE RIGUEUR *(to CÉLINE)*: And the sooner the better!

ANTOINE *(aside)*: My sentiments exactly! *(To MADAME DE RIGUEUR.)* Madame...

(He approaches her as CÉLINE *moves off, left.)*

MADAME DE RIGUEUR *(nodding politely)*: Monsieur...

ANTOINE: No time like the present...

MADAME DE RIGUEUR: Quite...

ANTOINE: Now this won't hurt a bit...

(He throws his arms around her neck and plants a kiss on her cheek.)

CÉLINE *(looking on in horror, as MADAME DE RIGUEUR screams)*: Oh!

ANTOINE *(to MADAME DE RIGUEUR)*: Let's let bygones be bygones, shall we?

MADAME DE RIGUEUR *(recovering her aplomb)*: You... You beast! You... You...

(She slaps him just as LECOUQUE *appears at the door, left.)*

ANTOINE *(recoiling)*: Again?

LECOUQUE *(entering)*: Oh my!... *(Solicitously, to* MADAME DE RIGUEUR.*)* Madame de Rigueur...

ANTOINE *(aside)*: Who?

MADAME DE RIGUEUR *(to* LECOUQUE*)*: What kind of depraved little games are you playing?

LECOUQUE: Me, madame?

MADAME DE RIGUEUR: Here! In your house! An utter stranger... A vulgar debauchee... A... a pervert!

LECOUQUE: But madame...

MADAME DE RIGUEUR *(pushing him aside)*: Out of my way, monsieur! I'm taking my business elsewhere!

LECOUQUE: But... But...

*(*MADAME DE RIGUEUR *stalks out, upstage.)*

CÉLINE: Oh!

LECOUQUE *(to* ANTOINE*)*: Now look what you've done!

*(*MADAME DE RIGUEUR *reappears at the door.)*

MADAME DE RIGUEUR: After I get my tiara!... This afternoon, understand?

(She stalks out once again.)

ANTOINE *(to* LECOUQUE*)*: But... I thought she was your wife...

LECOUQUE: You thought... You thought...

ANTOINE: Anyway, that one doesn't count, monsieur!... I mean, we agreed... Madame Lecouque...

LECOUQUE *(not wanting* CÉLINE *to hear)*: Yes, yes... For heaven's sake...

ANTOINE: Well? Where is she? It's time I met her...

LECOUQUE: She's not here, if you must know... She's out... At the police station...

ANTOINE: Oh... I'm sorry...

LECOUQUE: Looking for her handbag...

ANTOINE: Well then, she won't be long. I can wait... I'm in no hurry... *(He looks longingly at* CÉLINE.*)* No hurry at all... *(To* CÉLINE.*)* Am I, mademoiselle?

CÉLINE *(coyly lowering her eyes)*: I... I'm sure I don't know, monsieur...

LECOUQUE *(looking at them, back and forth, aside)*: What on earth are those two up do? *(To ANTOINE.)* I'm sorry, monsieur... She won't be back until two, and... and we're very busy! *(To CÉLINE.)* Aren't we, Céline?

CÉLINE: Oh no, Papa... We're not busy at all! Only Madame de Rigueur...

LECOUQUE: Yes we are! Don't contradict me!

CÉLINE *(naively)*: We are?

LECOUQUE *(pointing toward the door, right, to CÉLINE)*: Now you'd better get back to the shop...

CÉLINE: But Papa...

LECOUQUE: And don't come out unless I ring for you... *(He picks up the bell on the work table and gives a little jingle.)* Understand?

(CÉLINE, sighing, starts to leave, right.)

ANTOINE *(stopping her)*: No, no... You needn't... I'll go, mademoiselle... *(To LECOUQUE.)* Much as I hate to leave you, monsieur...

LECOUQUE: No doubt...

ANTOINE *(to LECOUQUE)*: Because to know you is to... *(Turning subtly toward CÉLINE.)* to love you...

LECOUQUE: I'm sure...

ANTOINE: But I'll be back... *(To LECOUQUE.)* At two o'clock, monsieur... To take care of our... unfinished business...

LECOUQUE: Yes, yes...

ANTOINE *(to CÉLINE, bowing)*: Mademoiselle... *(To LECOUQUE.)* Monsieur...

(He exits, upstage.)

CÉLINE *(after a brief pause)*: Who was that nice young gentleman, Papa?

LECOUQUE *(pointing to the door, upstage)*: Him?

CÉLINE: Yes... I'm sure he's never been here before... At least, I've never seen him!... *(Coyly.)* What could he want to speak with you about, I wonder?

LECOUQUE: Business, my dear... You heard him... Business...

CÉLINE *(with a note of good-natured sarcasm)*: My, my! I could have sworn it was for... Well, something else!

LECOUQUE: Oh?

CÉLINE: Yes... Why, after all, he kissed Madame de Rigueur because he thought she was Mamma! Surely that must mean something!

LECOUQUE *(trying to make light of it, shrugging)*: Well... Not necessarily...

CÉLINE: Come now, Papa... You don't have to pretend. I know all about it! Really, I do!

LECOUQUE: You do?

CÉLINE: Of course! Why, it's as plain as day! You didn't think you could fool me, did you? I can tell a suitor when I see one!

LECOUQUE: A suitor?... Him?

CÉLINE: And if you must know, Papa... He's really the nicest one you've ever brought to meet me!

LECOUQUE: What?

CÉLINE: Why, he's charming, and... and clever, and...

LECOUQUE: But... Wait just a minute...

CÉLINE: ...and terribly attractive! Oh yes, Papa! I'm sure... I'm simply sure I'm going to fall in love with him!

LECOUQUE *(aside)*: That's all I need! *(Aloud.)* He's... I'm telling you... He's not a suitor!

CÉLINE: Tsk tsk tsk! *(Shaking her finger at him.)* Papa... Papa...

LECOUQUE: But he's not! He's... he's...

CÉLINE: Yes?

LECOUQUE: He's... he's just someone who rides the tram, that's all!... And... *(Deciding to tell all.)* And he stroked your mother's foot... Because he thought it was his dog...

CÉLINE *(incredulous)*: What?

LECOUQUE: And if she doesn't let him kiss her... Just one little kiss... Then two men will be standing face to face, with drawn swords!... There! You wanted to know the truth... Now I hope you're satisfied!

CÉLINE *(sighing)*: Really, Papa! That's the most preposterous... Why on earth don't you want me to know he's a suitor?

LECOUQUE: But my dear child, I assure you... He's no such thing! I'm telling you...

CÉLINE *(pointing to her heart)*: And this tells me that he is!

LECOUQUE: "This..."? This what?

CÉLINE: My heart!

LECOUQUE: Your... your... *(At a loss for words.)* Oh... *(Beginning to lose patience.)* Get back to the shop, I told you!... And take your heart with you!

CÉLINE: But...

LECOUQUE *(mumbling)*: Your heart... And don't come out unless I ring for you!

CÉLINE: Yes, Papa!

(She exits, right.)

LECOUQUE: Her heart... That's all I need!... A young good-for-nothing!... And a painter, no less! Without a sou to his name, I suppose!...

(MADAME LECOUQUE appears, upstage, obviously out of patience.)

MADAME LECOUQUE *(entering)*: Well that was a fine waste of time!

LECOUQUE: Hildegarde!

(She takes off her hat and coat and lays them on one of the chairs, left.)

MADAME LECOUQUE: A wild goose chase!... The police were absolutely no help at all!

LECOUQUE *(trying to get her attention)*: My love...

MADAME LECOUQUE: I don't know what this city is coming to!

LECOUQUE: My love... While you were gone...

(He holds up her handbag.)

MADAME LECOUQUE: My... Where on earth did you...

(She takes it from him, examining the contents.)

LECOUQUE: A young man brought it back... A nice young man... Very nice... *(Aside.)* Now or never! *(Aloud.)* Really... Terribly nice...

MADAME LECOUQUE: How... nice! I hope you gave him a reward for his trouble.

LECOUQUE: Well, no...

MADAME LECOUQUE: Oh, Gustave! You should have... At least a franc or two...

LECOUQUE: Yes... Well... It wasn't exactly money he was after... *(Aside.)* Unfortunately! *(Aloud.)* That is...

MADAME LECOUQUE: That is...?

LECOUQUE: In fact... *(Forcing a laugh.)* You'll never believe it, Hildegarde... He's... He's the same young man...

MADAME LECOUQUE: What same young man?

LECOUQUE: The... the one you... you met last night... In the tram...

MADAME LECOUQUE: What?

LECOUQUE: Isn't that a coincidence?

MADAME LECOUQUE: Coincidence my foot! It's a scandal!

LECOUQUE *(still laughing)*: "My foot..." Her foot! That's a good one! Your foot...

MADAME LECOUQUE *(ignoring his remarks)*: Here, in this house! That... that...

LECOUQUE: But really, Hildegarde...

MADAME LECOUQUE: And you let him... You... You mean you didn't throw him out on his ear?

LECOUQUE: But I'm telling you... He explained... It wasn't his fault... He... he thought you were his dog...

MADAME LECOUQUE: He what?

LECOUQUE: I mean, your foot... He thought your foot was his dog... His pekingese...

MADAME LECOUQUE: He thought...

LECOUQUE: On account of the fur... Your shoe... With the fur...

MADAME LECOUQUE: Now I've heard everything! And you believed him?

LECOUQUE: Well, yes... I'm sure... I mean, if you saw him you would believe him too...

MADAME LECOUQUE: Heaven forbid!

LECOUQUE: Poor chap!... He... he didn't know what to say... He was all apologies... "Oh please, monsieur!... Please, tell madame how dreadfully sorry I am..."

MADAME LECOUQUE: Indeed!

LECOUQUE: That's what he said... "Dreadfully sorry..."

MADAME LECOUQUE: Hmm!

LECOUQUE: "...and that I hope she can find it in her heart to forgive me!"

MADAME LECOUQUE *(weakening)*: Oh?

LECOUQUE: Really, it was pathetic...

MADAME LECOUQUE: Well...

LECOUQUE: And after all, it wasn't his fault...

MADAME LECOUQUE: No, I suppose you're right... "To err is human..."

LECOUQUE *(relieved, sighing)*: My sentiments exactly!... "And to forgive..."

MADAME LECOUQUE *(hardening her position)*: Just don't let him show his face in my house again!

LECOUQUE: What?

MADAME LECOUQUE: I can't be responsible for what I might do!

LECOUQUE: But... but... he's coming back... At two o'clock... He said so...

MADAME LECOUQUE: He's what? What in heaven's name for?... What possible reason...

LECOUQUE: To beg you to forgive him... To hear it from your own lips, Hildegarde... And to ask you... To ask you... *(Aside.)* Good God, she'll never...

MADAME LECOUQUE: To ask me what?

LECOUQUE: To ask you to give him... to give him... something...

MADAME LECOUQUE: And what, may I ask? *(Sarcastically.)* The reward?

LECOUQUE: No, no, my love... A... a kiss... Just a little one...

MADAME LECOUQUE *(recoiling)*: I beg your... You're out of your mind! Give him a—

LECOUQUE *(interrupting)*: No, no... I meant... To let him give you... To let him... You don't have to do a thing... Just stand there and let him...

MADAME LECOUQUE: Gustave! You can't be serious!

LECOUQUE: Please, Hildegarde! For me!... Just a little one...

MADAME LECOUQUE: Never! Of all the—

LECOUQUE: But why not? At your age, what's the harm? That is...

MADAME LECOUQUE *(ready to slap him, but controlling her temper)*: Oh!... *(She moves upstage.)* Just like that! Kiss a man I've never met... An absolute stranger...

LECOUQUE *(as if giving her a convincing argument)*: But... but he brought back your handbag!

MADAME LECOUQUE: My handbag be... *(Moving down left.)* Would I have to kiss every man who brought back my handbag?

LECOUQUE: No, no... It's just that...

MADAME LECOUQUE *(sarcastically)*: Thank heavens it wasn't my valise! I can imagine...

LECOUQUE: It's just that, this one...

MADAME LECOUQUE *(regaining her composure, beginning to suspect something)*: Gustave, there's more to this than meets the eye!

LECOUQUE *(innocently)*: More, my love? More what?

MADAME LECOUQUE: Now stop pretending! What is this all about?

LECOUQUE *(after a pause, resigning himself, sighing)*: Well, if I must... Yes, you're right... There *is* more... Much more!

(He pauses again.)

MADAME LECOUQUE *(waiting)*: Well?

LECOUQUE: Either you kiss him or he challenges me to a duel! There! Now you know...

(There is another pause while MADAME LECOUQUE *waits for him to continue.)*

MADAME LECOUQUE: So?

LECOUQUE: "So?"

MADAME LECOUQUE: Is that all? A duel?... People fight them all the time!

LECOUQUE: Yes, people... But... but...

MADAME LECOUQUE: But what? Teach him a lesson!... You're not afraid, are you?

LECOUQUE: Afraid? A Lecouque?... Of course I'm not afraid!... Was I afraid when I served my country? Was I afraid when I faced death in the National Guard... Every day... On weekends... No, Hildegarde! I'm not afraid!... Not for me... Not for myself... I don't care about myself... But you, Hildegarde... And Céline... *(Growing more and more emotional.)* To leave you both... defenseless, unprotected...

MADAME LECOUQUE *(softening)*: Gustave...

LECOUQUE: Two waifs, alone... On this sea of degradation and corruption we call Paris... Flotsam and jetsam... My wife and my daughter...

MADAME LECOUQUE: Gustave, dearest...

LECOUQUE: And my business... The thought of leaving this nice little business, after all my work... Just when things are beginning to... Now that you're no longer... *(Abruptly changing the line of reasoning.)* I mean... At least, if I were rich... If I'd already made my fortune... Why, I wouldn't think twice... *(He makes a few heroic passes with an imaginary sword.)* Just like that! As long as I thought that you... and she...

(He chokes up with emotion.)

MADAME LECOUQUE *(touched)*: Gustave, please...

LECOUQUE: But I know how much you both need me... I know that I still have some use on this earth...

MADAME LECOUQUE: Of course you do, dearest... Of course you do...

LECOUQUE *(simply)*: Thank you...

MADAME LECOUQUE: And I want to do anything I can, believe me...

LECOUQUE: Then you mean you'll...

MADAME LECOUQUE: It's just that... Letting a strange man kiss me!... It's unheard of!... It's... it's...

LECOUQUE: But I'll be there... I'll be watching...

MADAME LECOUQUE: That's even worse!

LECOUQUE: I mean, it's not as if you're doing it behind my back...

MADAME LECOUQUE *(sighing)*: Still...

LECOUQUE: Really my love... You're making a mountain out of a molehill... Just make believe it's New Year's Day... Or your birthday... Or something... And a gentleman comes up to you and wants to wish you a—

MADAME LECOUQUE *(interrupting)*: A stranger? An absolute stranger?

LECOUQUE: Well, make believe he's not! Make believe it's the... the grocer...

MADAME LECOUQUE: What?

LECOUQUE: Please, Hildegarde! For me... *(Pointing toward the door, right.)* For her... For... for us!

MADAME LECOUQUE *(sighing)*: Oh, Gustave! I'll... I'll try... *(*LECOUQUE *heaves a sigh of relief.)* Really, I'll do my best...

LECOUQUE: Thank you, my love! I knew I could count on you.

MADAME LECOUQUE: Just give me a minute to put away my things...

(She picks up her hat and coat, and exits, left.)

LECOUQUE: Well... So far, so good...

*(*ANTOINE *appears at the door, upstage.)*

ANTOINE *(entering)*: Five minutes to two!... *(Noticing* LECOUQUE.*)* You can see I'm prompt, monsieur...

LECOUQUE *(sarcastically)*: Yes, I'm delighted!

ANTOINE: Punctuality is a virtue!... Well, is madame... Has she returned, monsieur?

LECOUQUE *(curtly)*: I'll go tell her you're here.

(He moves toward the door, left.)

ANTOINE *(stopping him)*: And mademoiselle, monsieur?

LECOUQUE: Mademoiselle who?

ANTOINE: Mademoiselle... Your daughter...

LECOUQUE: What about her?

ANTOINE: Is she at home too?

LECOUQUE: She's at work, monsieur... Just where she should be!

ANTOINE: Ah! Delightful creature... As industrious as she is beautiful!... An angel, monsieur... An angel...

LECOUQUE: Yes... Quite... *(Trying to move toward the door.)* Now, if you'll excuse me... I'll go get my wife...

ANTOINE *(holding him back)*: Perhaps you would like me to paint her portrait, monsieur? A beauty like her...

LECOUQUE: My wife?... You must be joking!

ANTOINE: No, no... Your daughter... In oils, of course...

LECOUQUE: For forty francs?· No thank you!

ANTOINE: For nothing, monsieur! For you, free of charge... Professional courtesy...

LECOUQUE: Thank you just the same! Not even if you pay me!

ANTOINE (*offended*): Oh...

LECOUQUE: Day after day, sitting after sitting... I have no intention of seeing you settle in!

ANTOINE: But...

LECOUQUE: Now, if you don't mind, I'll go get my wife, and you'll proceed with the business at hand! And then you'll leave!

ANTOINE: Very good, monsieur.

LECOUQUE: And for goodness' sake, remember she has something of a temper.

ANTOINE: "Something," monsieur? (*With a sardonic smile.*) You'll recall, I've been treated to rather ample proof!

LECOUQUE: Yes, well... Just don't do anything to make her lose it! No emotion... Nothing... No feeling, understand?

ANTOINE: Of course, monsieur! What do you take me for?

LECOUQUE: And whatever you do, keep your mouth shut!

ANTOINE: Indeed! You can rest assured...

LECOUQUE (*at the door, left*): No comments... Not a word...
(*He exits.*)

ANTOINE: Not a word... My lips are sealed... (*He moves right, toward the work table, sighing.*) Besides, who cares? It's not the mother I want... It's... It's that delightful creature... (*Gazing lovingly toward the door, right.*) In there... Just a few feet away... (*He begins to tremble.*) Just the thought of it makes me... Oh my! Look how I'm trembling... And to think, just a ring of this bell... Just a little tinkle, and she would walk through that door... (*He goes over, about to pick up the bell, but hesitates.*) Oh no, Antoine! You mustn't... You wouldn't dare... If you do... (*He picks it up in his trembling hand and, without meaning to, makes it ring.*) Oh my! I did!... (*He claps his other hand over the bell, but as soon as he removes it, he inadvertently rings it again.*) Oh...

(CÉLINE *appears at the door, right, holding a flowered tiara.*)

CÉLINE (*entering*): Did you ring for me, Papa?... (*Noticing* ANTOINE.) Oh, monsieur...

ANTOINE (*absentmindedly putting the bell in his pocket*): Mademoiselle...

CÉLINE: I thought my father...

ANTOINE: No, no... It was me... It was I... *(Bumbling.)* I mean... You must be surprised to see me, mademoiselle.

CÉLINE: Surprised?... Not at all, monsieur! I know all about it!

ANTOINE: Oh? You do?

CÉLINE: Of course! Papa tried terribly hard not to let on...

ANTOINE: Yes, I should think...

CÉLINE *(laughing)*: You should have heard him, monsieur... But I guessed... I always do, you know...

ANTOINE: "Always..." You mean, this... this has happened before?

CÉLINE: I should say!

ANTOINE *(aside)*: My heavens! *(To* CÉLINE.*)* Very often?

CÉLINE: Oh yes! *(Laughing.)* I've lost count...

ANTOINE: You've lost...

CÉLINE: But it's always the same, monsieur... They come in and they talk with Papa...

ANTOINE: And your mother...?

CÉLINE: Oh yes, Mamma too... And I'm never supposed to know that they're asking to marry me!

ANTOINE *(with a start)*: That they're asking...

CÉLINE: Just like you, monsieur... *(Coyly.)* But I'm not supposed to know!

ANTOINE *(nonplussed)*: Just like... *(Aside.)* Now there's an idea!

CÉLINE: But of course, I always do!

ANTOINE: No!... You mean, we didn't fool you? You... You knew all along that... that I love you, mademoiselle? That I'm head over heels...

CÉLINE: Really, monsieur! It's never very hard to tell!

ANTOINE *(aside)*: With all that practice!

CÉLINE *(very matter-of-factly)*: Well, I'd better be getting back, monsieur... Papa will be angry... *(Holding up the tiara.)* He promised this for today... This afternoon...

ANTOINE *(stopping her)*: What a lovely bouquet!

CÉLINE: It's not a bouquet, silly! It's a tiara! You wear it...

ANTOINE: Oh, of course...

CÉLINE: Navy blue tea roses... Papa says they have to sing...

ANTOINE *(taking the tiara, admiringly)*: And to think... With your own two hands...

(He kisses it.)

CÉLINE: Monsieur! What are you doing?

ANTOINE: With your own little fingers... *(He kisses it again.)* Who wouldn't be pretty with a... *(Searching for the word.)* a "tarara" like that?... Even... *(Placing it on his own head.)* Voilà! *(CÉLINE begins to laugh.)* What's so funny?

CÉLINE: You've put it on upside down, monsieur!

ANTOINE: Upside down?... What did I tell you? Head over heels!

CÉLINE *(taking the tiara from his head, standing on tiptoes)*: Here... Let me... *(She sits down on the loveseat.)* Get down...

ANTOINE *(kneeling down in front of her, rather facetiously)*: You see? I'm already throwing myself at your feet!

(CÉLINE adjusts the tiara on his head.)

CÉLINE *(laughing)*: There! That's perfect!

(Just at that moment, LECOUQUE enters, left, followed by MADAME LECOUQUE, whom he is holding by the hand.)

(The following two exclamations are simultaneous.)

LECOUQUE: What on earth...

MADAME LECOUQUE: Céline!

(The following two exclamations are simultaneous.)

ANTOINE: Oh, my goodness!

CÉLINE: Mamma! Papa!

(ANTOINE quickly gets to his feet, still wearing the tiara.)

ANTOINE *(bowing)*: Madame... Monsieur...

(The following two exclamations are simultaneous.)

MADAME LECOUQUE: What do you think you're...

LECOUQUE: Madame de Rigueur's...

(LECOUQUE pulls the tiara from ANTOINE's head.)

LECOUQUE: Give me that!... Her tea roses...

MADAME LECOUQUE: Oh!

LECOUQUE: Look! They're all crumpled!

MADAME LECOUQUE *(to CÉLINE)*: You should be ashamed of yourself, Céline!

CÉLINE: But...

MADAME LECOUQUE *(pointing right)*: Now get back in there at once!

LECOUQUE *(handing* CÉLINE *the tiara)*: And take care of this! They've got to sing, understand? They've got to sing!

CÉLINE: But Mamma...

MADAME LECOUQUE: No "buts," young lady! *(Pointing.)* Out!

CÉLINE *(sighing)*: Oh...

(She grudgingly exits, right, leaving the door slightly ajar and eavesdropping, unnoticed by the others.)

LECOUQUE *(after a brief pause, to* ANTOINE*)*: Now then, monsieur... Let's proceed with the business at hand...

ANTOINE *(with a foolish little laugh)*: That's rather good, monsieur...

LECOUQUE: Please?

ANTOINE: "The business at hand..." At hand, indeed!... *(Giving himself a little slap on both cheeks.)* Very good...

MADAME LECOUQUE *(resisting the urge to slap him, aside)*: Idiot!

LECOUQUE: Monsieur, don't be impertinent!

ANTOINE: Oh, sorry...

LECOUQUE: Madame is ready!

ANTOINE *(to* LECOUQUE, *whispering)*: I thought you said she was pretty!

(The two men continue their exchange in a whisper.)

LECOUQUE: "Ish," I said... "Ish"...

ANTOINE: Even "ish"!... I mean, really...

LECOUQUE: Please, no comments... You promised...

ANTOINE: Quite... *(Aloud, to* MADAME LECOUQUE.*)* Madame, first, let me assure you that I'm not what you take me for...

MADAME LECOUQUE *(offering her cheek)*: Please, let's get it over with!

ANTOINE: I'm really a fine young man...

MADAME LECOUQUE: No doubt!

LECOUQUE *(aside to* ANTOINE*)*: No speeches, I said!

ANTOINE *(to* MADAME LECOUQUE*)*: Believe me... You'll see...

MADAME LECOUQUE *(losing patience)*: Monsieur!

ANTOINE: And that's why I have the honor...

LECOUQUE: Please...

ANTOINE: ...of asking for the hand of your daughter in marriage!

(The following two exclamations are simultaneous.)

MADAME LECOUQUE: My daughter...

LECOUQUE: What?

MADAME LECOUQUE *(indignantly)*: You?... *(She slaps him in the face.)* The nerve!

ANTOINE: Oh!

CÉLINE *(poking her head out, unseen by the others)*: Oh dear!

MADAME LECOUQUE *(moving upstage)*: That, monsieur, is the only hand you'll get!

ANTOINE *(rubbing his cheek, crossing right, fuming)*: Again?... Oh no! That's the last straw!... The last...

LECOUQUE: Monsieur...

ANTOINE *(to MADAME LECOUQUE)*: Madame, if you weren't a lady... *(Correcting.)* A woman...

MADAME LECOUQUE: I beg your—

ANTOINE *(ranting)*: A man, good God!... Is there a man in this house?

LECOUQUE *(trying to calm him)*: Monsieur...

ANTOINE: You!

(He gives his face a resounding slap.)

CÉLINE *(aside)*: Oh! Papa...

LECOUQUE *(furious)*: You... You dare...

MADAME LECOUQUE: Gustave... He hit you!

LECOUQUE: I know, damn it! I know!... *(To* ANTOINE.*)* Monsieur, this means a duel!

MADAME LECOUQUE *(to* ANTOINE*)*: That's right! *(To* LECOUQUE.*)* Teach him a lesson!

ANTOINE: A duel, monsieur?

LECOUQUE: To the death!

MADAME LECOUQUE *(echoing)*: To the death!

CÉLINE *(aside)*: To the death?

ANTOINE: To the death?

LECOUQUE: A Lecouque, monsieur, defends his honor with his blood!

MADAME LECOUQUE *(to* ANTOINE*)*: That's right, monsieur! His blood...

ANTOINE *(aside)*: Yes... Or mine...

CÉLINE *(aside)*: Oh my, oh my...

LECOUQUE *(very correct, to* ANTOINE*)*: Now if monsieur will excuse me, I'll go get the weapons!

MADAME LECOUQUE *(to* LECOUQUE*)*: Yes, Gustave... The weapons...

*(*LECOUQUE *and* MADAME LECOUQUE *exit, left.)*

ANTOINE *(alone)*: Hmm! Maybe I was a little hasty...

CÉLINE *(bursting out from behind the door)*: Well, monsieur! Very nice!

ANTOINE: Mademoiselle...

CÉLINE: A duel with Papa! That's a fine way to ask to marry me, I must say! What ever will you do?

ANTOINE: Oh, don't worry about me! I can take care of myself! *(He dramatically assumes the "en garde" position.)*

CÉLINE: Yes, but you wouldn't kill Papa, I hope...

ANTOINE: Oh, I...

CÉLINE: Because if you did, you know... Well then, I'd never be able to marry you...

ANTOINE *(reflecting)*: No... That's true...

CÉLINE: I mean... Never! Really!

ANTOINE: But then again, if he kills me...

CÉLINE: We wouldn't be much better off, monsieur, would we?

ANTOINE: No...

CÉLINE: You, especially...

ANTOINE: Quite!

CÉLINE: Of course, you could always apologize...

ANTOINE: I could do what?

CÉLINE: Apologize... Tell him you're sorry...

ANTOINE: A Falsetto, mademoiselle?

CÉLINE: A what?

ANTOINE: A Falsetto... That's my name... My father was Italian.

CÉLINE: Oh, I didn't know...

ANTOINE: You want me to apologize? Swallow my pride?

CÉLINE: For me, monsieur... Monsieur Falsetto... That is... *(Suggestively.)* For us...

ANTOINE: Well, as long as you put it that way, I suppose...

(LECOUQUE bursts in, left, carrying a tray with two cups, one white and the other blue.)

LECOUQUE: All right, monsieur! *(Suddenly noticing CÉLINE.)* Céline! I thought I told you...

(He points peremptorily toward the door, right.)

CÉLINE *(docilely)*: Yes, Papa... I'm going... *(Aside, to* ANTOINE, *as she leaves.)* Remember... For us...

(She exits, right.)

LECOUQUE *(very formally)*: Monsieur...

ANTOINE *(nodding)*: Monsieur...

LECOUQUE: I'm sure you understand how my honor has been attacked...

ANTOINE: Well, actually, I thought we might—

LECOUQUE: ...and that one of us must vanish from the face of the earth!

ANTOINE: Oh? I thought... I thought...

LECOUQUE: You thought, monsieur?

ANTOINE: That... that perhaps we might come to an... an amicable understanding...

LECOUQUE: Understanding?... A Lecouque?... Ha ha! *(Derisively.)* You must be mad!

ANTOINE: Well...

LECOUQUE: To the death, monsieur! To the death!... Now then, as the offended party I have the right to choose the weapons... I've chosen a duel with cups of milk.

ANTOINE *(bewildered, with a laugh)*: What? We're going to drink milk?

LECOUQUE: Don't joke, monsieur! This is serious!... I've scratched the sulphur from seventy-two matches into one of these cups...

ANTOINE: Oh? Which one?

LECOUQUE *(ignoring his question)*: The one who drinks it will have long, horrible convulsions, until he drops dead.

ANTOINE *(almost facetiously)*: Good heavens! I've met my match!

LECOUQUE: Please! I told you... This is serious!

ANTOINE: Sorry...

LECOUQUE: Well, are you ready?

ANTOINE: Excuse me, monsieur, but... A duel is one thing, but... I'm really not thirsty...

LECOUQUE: You mean, you're afraid?

ANTOINE: No... It's just that I promised your daughter, monsieur... *(LECOUQUE gives him a quizzical look.)* I promised her I would try to settle our differences...

LECOUQUE: Impossible, monsieur! What's done is done!

(He places the try on the end table near the loveseat.)

ANTOINE: Even if it meant that I... *(Clearing his throat.)* That is...

LECOUQUE *(curtly)*: Unacceptable, monsieur! No apologies accepted!... Now then, I'm the offended party, so I have my choice... I take the white cup. Here, you swallow the blue one...

(He turns the tray with the blue cup toward ANTOINE.)

ANTOINE *(recoiling)*: Ha! You're out of your mind!

LECOUQUE: You refuse?

ANTOINE: Of course I do! What do you take me for?... *(Mimicking.)* "You swallow the blue one!"

LECOUQUE: That's what I said...

ANTOINE: No, thank you!... You scratch the matches, and you tell me which one to drink! That's a good one!

LECOUQUE: But...

ANTOINE: I choose the white one too!... *(Turning the tray.)* Here, you swallow the blue one!

LECOUQUE: But protocol... I'm the offended—

ANTOINE: Protocol be damned!

LECOUQUE: Oh! Have you no sense of honor, monsieur? No sense... No sense...

ANTOINE: Too much sense, thank you!

LECOUQUE: I see! In other words—

ANTOINE: In other words, if you insist on this... this duel...

LECOUQUE: I do!

ANTOINE: Then I insist we let someone else do the choosing for us... A third party, monsieur... With no axe to grind...

LECOUQUE: Very well... I'll call my wife...

(He begins to leave.)

ANTOINE: Your... *(Stopping him.)* Oh no!... No, no, no!

LECOUQUE: Monsieur?

ANTOINE: She helped you scratch the matches! She knows... She... No, no! I'd prefer your daughter!

LECOUQUE: Céline?... Hmm!... Well... *(Aside.)* Blood is thicker than water... *(Aloud.)* I suppose... *(Aside.):* She'll make the right choice... *(Aloud.)* All right, monsieur! My daughter!

ANTOINE: Fine!

LECOUQUE: But not a word to her, understand?

ANTOINE: Not a word!

LECOUQUE: I'll call her... *(He looks around on the work table for the bell.)* Where the devil is that bell?

ANTOINE *(looking around)*: The bell, monsieur?

LECOUQUE: It's usually on the table...

ANTOINE: Yes, I remember...

(He moves around, looking for the bell with LECOUQUE. As he does so, it jingles in his pocket.)

LECOUQUE: Strange... I seem to hear it...

ANTOINE: So do I...

LECOUQUE: But I don't see it...

ANTOINE: I know I had it, but...

LECOUQUE: It must be somewhere...

ANTOINE *(stopping to listen)*: Listen... It stopped...

(He moves around again, stopping several times, LECOUQUE follows him, trying to detect the source of the sound. Finally the light dawns and he stops ANTOINE.)

LECOUQUE *(pointing to the offending pocket)*: Monsieur!

ANTOINE *(feeling his pocket and taking out the bell)*: Now what is it doing in there?

LECOUQUE *(pulling it away)*: Give me that!

(He rings it. CÉLINE appears at the door, right.)

CÉLINE: Did someone ring?

LECOUQUE: Come here, Céline...

CÉLINE *(joining him)*: Yes, Papa...

LECOUQUE: Monsieur has agreed to do us the honor of accepting a cup of milk... *(Pointing to the tray.)* Pure, delicious milk... Please be good enough to serve us.

CÉLINE: Then you mean... You've made up?

ANTOINE: In a manner of speaking.

CÉLINE *(to* ANTOINE*)*: Which one would you like, monsieur?

LECOUQUE *(aside to* ANTOINE*)*: Not a word!

ANTOINE *(to* CÉLINE, *as offhand as possible)*: Oh, it really doesn't matter, mademoiselle... You decide... *(Raising his eyes to heaven, aside.)* Don't let her be a widow before she's a wife!

LECOUQUE *(to* CÉLINE*)*: Yes, you decide... *(Raising his eyes, aside.)* Don't let her be an orphan!

*(*CÉLINE *takes the blue cup.)*

(The following two exclamations are simultaneous.)

ANTOINE: Good God!

LECOUQUE: Oh my!

(Both men watch uneasily as CÉLINE *seems uncertain whom to serve first. Finally, she moves toward* LECOUQUE *with the cup.)*

LECOUQUE *(to* CÉLINE *as inconspicuously as possible, waving her off toward* ANTOINE*)*: Pssst... Pssst...

CÉLINE *(to* ANTOINE*)*: Here, monsieur... Guests first...

ANTOINE *(taking the cup, aside)*: Ay ay ay!... *(Aloud.)* Thank you, mademoiselle... *(Aside.)* My angel... of death!

CÉLINE *(aside)*: Milk in the afternoon! Of all things...

LECOUQUE *(smiling)*: Our pleasure, monsieur! *(Taking the white cup and raising it.)* To your health, young man!

CÉLINE *(aside)*: Anyway, they've made up, and that's all that matters!

ANTOINE *(raising his cup)*: To yours, old friend!

(He pauses.)

LECOUQUE *(waiting, to* ANTOINE*)*: Well, aren't you going to drink it?

ANTOINE: I... It's... I'm not sure I should... It's bad for my liver...

CÉLINE: Nonsense, monsieur! Milk is good for you!

ANTOINE *(aside)*: Sometimes...

LECOUQUE *(to* ANTOINE*)*: See? You heard her...

ANTOINE: Besides, there's a fly in it...

CÉLINE *(looking)*: Where? In our milk?

ANTOINE: Well, I thought... I'm sure I saw one... A big one... Black...

CÉLINE: You couldn't have, monsieur! We don't have any!

ANTOINE: Oh... *(Aside.)* No harm trying...

LECOUQUE: Well, bottoms up!

ANTOINE *(sardonically)*: Cheers!

LECOUQUE: Chin chin, and all that...

ANTOINE *(touched, wiping away a tear)*: Ah yes... Chin-Chin... My little Chin-Chin...

CÉLINE *(to ANTOINE)*: Monsieur?

ANTOINE: My dog, mademoiselle... I was thinking about my dog...

CÉLINE *(aside)*: His dog?

ANTOINE *(to LECOUQUE)*: Excuse me, monsieur, but... Could you spare a sheet of paper?

LECOUQUE: What for?

ANTOINE: A few last minute arrangements... Before I... take my leave...

LECOUQUE: I suppose it's only right...

(He goes to his desk, down right, and puts down the white cup while assembling paper, pen and ink.)

CÉLINE *(surprised, to ANTOINE)*: Are you going somewhere, monsieur?

ANTOINE: Yes, I'm afraid so...

CÉLINE *(disillusioned)*: But where? You told me...

ANTOINE: I'm going... I'm going, mademoiselle, where the tea roses bloom forever...

CÉLINE: But... I thought you were a painter, monsieur... Not a florist...

ANTOINE: Yes, I am... That is, I was... Have been... Used to be... *(Shrugging.)* Whatever...

LECOUQUE *(at the desk, to ANTOINE)*: There you are, monsieur...

ANTOINE: Ah! Much obliged... *(Handing him the blue cup.)* Here, would you mind... *(He fumbles in his pocket for some coins.)* That's fifty centimes...

(He gives the coins to LECOUQUE.)

LECOUQUE: What for?

ANTOINE: Well, you'll have to get it notarized, and...

LECOUQUE: Oh, you didn't have to bother... *(Aside, pocketing the coins.)* Thoughtful chap!

(As ANTOINE *sits down at the desk,* LECOUQUE *inadvertently raises the blue cup to his lips, stops in horror as he realizes his error, and slips it back into* ANTOINE's *left hand as the latter begins to write with his right.)*

ANTOINE *(writing)*: "I, Antoine Falsetto, being of sane mind and sound body, hereby bequest my entire estate..."

CÉLINE *(aside)*: "Bequeath..." What on earth...

ANTOINE: "...all property and possessions to my faithful dog, Chin-Chin..."

(The following two exclamations are simultaneous.)

CÉLINE: What?

LECOUQUE: Monsieur?

ANTOINE: "...including my annual income of twenty-five thousand francs..."

LECOUQUE *(with a start, to* ANTOINE*)*: Your what?... Twenty-five thousand a year?

ANTOINE *(diffidently)*: Well, in round figures...

LECOUQUE: Why in heaven's name didn't you say so in the first place?

ANTOINE *(putting the cup to his lips)*: And now... *(With a dramatic gaze at* CÉLINE.*)* Farewell...

LECOUQUE *(trying to pull the cup away)*: For God's sake, don't drink that!

CÉLINE: But...

ANTOINE *(persisting)*: My honor, monsieur! My honor...

LECOUQUE: Twenty-five thousand... *(Calling.)* Hildegarde!... *(To* CÉLINE.*)* Help me...

CÉLINE: But...

LECOUQUE *(calling)*: Hildegarde! Hildegarde!

(They continue the tug-of-war, as MADAME LECOUQUE *appears, left.)*

MADAME LECOUQUE *(entering)*: Gustave... What are you...

LECOUQUE *(aside to* MADAME LECOUQUE, *pointing to* ANTOINE*)*: Twenty-five thousand... He has twenty-five thousand a year!

MADAME LECOUQUE *(aside to* LECOUQUE*)*: I don't believe it!

LECOUQUE *(to* ANTOINE*)*: Young man, my daughter is yours!

ANTOINE *(putting down the cup)*: She is?

CÉLINE: Oh, Papa...

LECOUQUE *(to* ANTOINE*)*: You're the son I've always dreamed of!

MADAME LECOUQUE *(to* ANTOINE*)*: A marriage made in heaven!

CÉLINE *(to* ANTOINE*)*: Oh monsieur... Monsieur...

ANTOINE: I... I don't know what to say... Monsieur... Madame...

LECOUQUE: Just say yes...

MADAME LECOUQUE: Say yes...

CÉLINE: Yes... Say yes...

ANTOINE *(enthusiastically)*: Yes!... Yes, yes!... *(Aside.)* It's really twenty-five hundred, but what's a zero more or less? *(To* LECOUQUE.*)* Father!... *(To* MADAME LECOUQUE.*)* Mother!...

MADAME LECOUQUE *(embracing him)*: Son!

CÉLINE *(coquettishly)*: Antoine!

ANTOINE *(aside)*: They'll find out soon enough...

CÉLINE *(to* LECOUQUE*)*: You see, Papa! I knew it all along!

MADAME LECOUQUE *(taking* ANTOINE *aside, in a whisper)*: When you have to talk money, Antoine, come see me...

LECOUQUE *(to* CÉLINE*)*: Knew it? Knew what?

MADAME LECOUQUE *(still whispering, to* ANTOINE*)*: Gustave... Monsieur is an absolute zero!

CÉLINE *(to* LECOUQUE*)*: That he was a suitor!

ANTOINE *(to* MADAME LECOUQUE, *whispering)*: Fine! *(Aside.)* I can use one! *(Holding out his hand to* CÉLINE, *who joins him.)* Céline...

MADAME LECOUQUE *(to* ANTOINE, *aloud)*: And now, son, I think you should collect what I owe you!

ANTOINE: Mother?

MADAME LECOUQUE: Two kisses, you dear boy! One for each slap!

(They all laugh, as ANTOINE *gives* CÉLINE *two kisses, one on each cheek.)*

ANTOINE: There!

MADAME LECOUQUE: No, no! Here I am... Over here...

ANTOINE: Oh... My mistake! It's so hard to tell the difference! *(LECOUQUE stifles a guffaw.)*

MADAME LECOUQUE: Really? *(Kissing him.)* Why you dear, sweet boy, you! *(To* LECOUQUE.*)* Isn't he sweet, Gustave?

LECOUQUE: Oh, I should say, my love! *(Aside, jovially.)* A liar, but sweet!

ANTOINE *(aside to* LECOUQUE, *laughing)*: Well... "Ish..."

LECOUQUE *(aside to* ANTOINE, *laughing)*: "Ish..."

ANTOINE *(aloud)*: There's one thing I'm sure of... I'll never stroke my Chin-Chin again in the tram... At least, not in the dark...

CÉLINE *(turning to* LECOUQUE, *puzzled)*: He'll never what?

MADAME LECOUQUE *(to* ANTOINE*)*: Your Chin-Chin indeed!... Your Chin-Chin my foot foot!

(They all laugh, except CÉLINE, *who continues to look on quizzically.)*

CÉLINE: Will somebody please tell me what is so funny?

LECOUQUE: I told you before... Your mother...

MADAME LECOUQUE: I was sitting in the tram...

ANTOINE: And I was with my dog...

(The three of them continue talking, all at once, trying to explain to a bewildered CÉLINE, *as the curtain slowly falls.)*

CURTAIN

A MATTER OF WIFE AND DEATH

(LA LETTRE CHARGÉE)

(1877)

Characters:

VAN LUST
GASTON
VIVIANE
JACQUELINE

Scene:

The drawing room in Viviane's Parisian apartment. Upstage center, a double door. Down left, another door. Down right, against the wall, a sewing cabinet. Midstage, left of center, a table and chair. On the table, pen and ink, stationery, envelopes, and a bell. Midstage, right of center, a loveseat. Next to it, a small end table. Other appropriate furnishings—lamps, pictures, etc.—ad lib.

At rise, GASTON *and* VIVIANE *are seated on the loveseat.* GASTON *is dozing.*

VIVIANE *(reading)*:
"Now, Poet, take thy lute. Come, kiss thy muse.
Tonight the burgeoning spring is newly born;
The wild rose blooms; the breeze blows forth the news;
And feathered wagtail, waiting for the morn,
Lights on the season's first green bough and thorn.
Now, Poet, take thy lute..."

(She stops as GASTON *emits a loud snore.)* Oh no! Not again!... Just look at him... *(To* GASTON, *softly.)* Gaston... Cousin dear... *(To the audience.)* I must say, for a man who's come all the way from Dunkerque to ask me to marry him... Three times... Well... *(With a sweeping gesture.)* There he is! Monsieur Gaston de Courvalin, member of the bar... *(With a little laugh,)* And clearly a man with no taste for poetry!

GASTON *(mumbling in his sleep)*: Exquisite... Scintillating...

VIVIANE *(shaking her head)*: And that's not his only fault, I'm afraid!... Oh, nothing really serious, heaven knows... But still, sometimes it's just so annoying I could scream!... The man has an absolute mania for big words!... Really, that's what it is! A mania!... And the longer the better!... Why, he used one yesterday... I thought it would never end! He opened his mouth and it just kept coming!... "Transubstantiationally," if you can believe it!... He simply can't speak simply... *(Laughing.)* As it were!

GASTON *(still dozing)*: A rhapsody... A dithyramb...

VIVIANE: Even in his sleep, poor dear! *(Turning back to him, reading.)*

"Now, Poet, take thy lute..."

(Getting up, to the audience.) Still, he has all kinds of excellent qualities... *(Laughing.)* A sound sleeper, for one thing!... And a heart of gold... Devoted, to a fault... *(Sighing.)* Yes, I suppose I really should marry him! I can't see any reason not to... *(GASTON emits another loud snore.)* No serious reason... Yes, this spring, I should think... If the weather holds up... *(Looking at him.)* Well, there's no sense reading to myself, I must say!

(She sits down again and raps the book on the end table.)

GASTON *(waking up suddenly)*: Hmm?... What?... Ah, Viviane... Concluded already?

VIVIANE: Yes... *(Wryly.)* I read quickly...

GASTON: I should say!

VIVIANE: Did you enjoy it?

GASTON: Prodigiously, my dear! Especially the termination!

VIVIANE: Beg pardon?

GASTON: The conclusion...

VIVIANE: Aha... You mean, the end?

GASTON: Why... yes...

VIVIANE *(to the audience)*: Case in point!

GASTON: You read so enthrallingly!

VIVIANE *(to the audience)*: And another!

GASTON: I could sit here and listen in perpetuity!

VIVIANE *(to the audience)*: And another!... *(To GASTON, good-naturedly.)* Oh, don't stop now! I'm sure you must have more!

GASTON: More?... More what?

VIVIANE: More of your "protracted verbiage," as someone I know might so aptly put it...

GASTON: More of my...

VIVIANE: Big words, my love! Really, it's a... a disease! You can't open your mouth without breaking out in a rash of the most long-winded, incomprehensible... *(Laughing.)* I'm afraid you're simply incurable, cousin dear!

GASTON *(somewhat abashed)*: But... Why, I never... I wasn't aware... That is, I suppose it's a characteristic I've become habituated to—

VIVIANE *(interrupting, wagging her finger)*: Gaston!

GASTON: I mean, a habit I've contracted...

VIVIANE: Better...

GASTON: ...as a professional exigency...

VIVIANE *(aside)*: Hopeless!

GASTON: We legal practitioners, after all... We do become adept at manipulating the lexicon... Even when the significance is debatable, and the concept less than pellucid...

VIVIANE *(aside, shrugging)*: No doubt!

GASTON: But... *(Speaking slowly and carefully.)* But from now on I'll be careful! You'll see, I'll watch myself like a hawk!... Anything to make you happy, Viviane!... Anything for the woman I want to make my wife!

VIVIANE: You're sweet!

GASTON *(still speaking with obvious care)*: And as long as we're on the subject... Tomorrow it will be two weeks since I left Dunkerque... This time, that is... Because the other two times... Well, I don't have to tell you...

VIVIANE: Yes...

GASTON *(beginning to forget himself)*: And I have no option but to vacate the premises and return posthaste to my juridical pursuits...

VIVIANE *(aside)*: Oh my...

GASTON: But preceding my departure... Prior to my leave-taking...

VIVIANE: Yes... Before you go...

GASTON: I would esteem myself fortunate indeed...

VIVIANE *(aside)*: Indeed!

GASTON: ...to have some incontrovertible indication that, on this occasion, my suit will not remain infecund...

VIVIANE *(aside)*: Good heavens! I don't believe it!

GASTON: When one loves as I do... Madly... Passionately...

VIVIANE *(wryly)*: Oh? Is that all? "Madly..." I would have thought...

GASTON: Unswervingly... Unremittingly... Indefatigably...

VIVIANE: Aha! That's more like it!... Well, cousin dear, I appreciate the attention... *(Grandiloquently.)* But I feel it my obligation to apprize you... to render you cognizant, that is... of the fact that, while you have been engaged in "manipulating the lexicon," a rival has been endeavoring to manipulate my affection! *(Aside.)* So there!

GASTON *(with a start)*: A rival? That's impossible!

VIVIANE: Oh? *(With a coy little pout.)* That's not very flattering!

GASTON: I mean... *(Babbling.)* I... I've come all the way from Dunkerque... I... Who... Who is he?

VIVIANE *(resuming her usual tone)*: As a matter of fact, I haven't the vaguest idea. Except that he's an American...

GASTON *(scandalized)*: A what?

VIVIANE: ...and that he sent me the most incredible letter, day before yesterday.

GASTON *(incredulous)*: No!

VIVIANE: Yes! *(Crossing left to the table, opening the drawer and holding up some papers.)* Listen... *(Reading.)* "Dear Viviane..."

GASTON *(aside)*: Impertinent!...

VIVIANE *(continuing)*: "You are a widow, and so am I..."

GASTON: Singular!... A widow?

VIVIANE: You know what he means... *(Reading.)* "You want to remarry, and so do I. You are in excellent health, and so am I..."

GASTON *(aside)*: Presumptuous!...

VIVIANE *(continuing)*: "So I don't see any reason why we shouldn't get together..."

GASTON: Piquant deduction, I must say!

VIVIANE *(continuing)*: "I'm not enclosing my picture because it isn't very flattering. But I can be seen any time you like, for the next two days, while I'm still in Paris. Please reply in care of the Hotel De Luxe, Room 124. Yours truly, Timothy Van Lust."

GASTON: Egregious!... Utterly...

VIVIANE *(reading)*: "P.S., I'm an American."

GASTON: I never would have guessed!

VIVIANE *(aside)*: Or even hazarded a conjecture!

GASTON: Of all things... It must be a prank, Viviane! Some buffoon's conception of a bit of jocular banter...

VIVIANE: Yes, well... If so, it's a prank in two parts.

GASTON: Two...?

VIVIANE: He sent me another letter yesterday.

GASTON: He did?

VIVIANE *(reading)*: "Dear Viviane, I can't understand why you haven't replied to mine of the twenty-sixth..."

GASTON: Obviously some madman... Most likely cyclothymic...

VIVIANE: "Cyclo..." Really, Gaston!... *(Shaking her head.)* "Cyclo..."

GASTON: Sorry, my dear! It just came out...

VIVIANE: Well, my goodness!... Put it back!

GASTON: Please... I'll try to be more careful! I'll watch myself... Like a hawk...

VIVIANE: Of course...

GASTON: You'll see... *(Speaking very carefully, taking the letters.)* Here, let me have those. A friend of mine is with the local police. I'll go have a word with him.

VIVIANE: Oh... If you would...

GASTON *(gradually reverting to form)*: I'm certain he'll be able to provide pertinent facts regarding any foreign nationals currently residing in the vicinity...

VIVIANE *(nodding)*: I'm sure...

GASTON: ...resulting, no doubt, in a abundance of details...

VIVIANE *(resigned)*: Yes...

GASTON: ...and a veritable plethora of information concerning your Monsieur... your Mister Timothy Van Lust...

VIVIANE *(good-naturedly, sighing)*: Gaston! You're impossible!

GASTON: Oh my... Did I do it again?

VIVIANE: I'm afraid so...

GASTON: I'm sorry...

VIVIANE: Good heavens! Do you think I want to marry a... a dictionary? Really, cousin dear! I'd jump out of my skin!

GASTON *(falling to his knees)*: But... But I love you, Viviane!... I... I love you!

VIVIANE *(with a little laugh)*: Now *that* I understand! Simple and direct...

GASTON: I... I've come all the way...

VIVIANE: Poor Gaston...

GASTON: I'll be careful... I'll watch myself...

VIVIANE: Like a hawk! I know...

GASTON: You'll see...

VIVIANE *(coyly)*: Well... All right, I'll forgive you... If you promise...

GASTON *(jumping to his feet)*: I do! I do!

VIVIANE: Good! Now be a dear... Run to the police station and see what you can find out about our friend...

GASTON: Instanter!

(He exits, upstage.)

VIVIANE *(shaking her head)*: He's right... He can't help it!... Oh well, I can get used to it, I suppose. *(Getting up.)* But I really must give him an answer today! Three trips, poor thing... And all the way from Dunkerque!... I simply can't continue this perpetual vacillation... This... *(Reflecting for a moment.)* Oh my! It's contagious!

(JACQUELINE enters, upstage, holding a large letter in one hand and an open register in the other.)

JACQUELINE *(at the door)*: Madame... There's a letter... With lots and lots of stamps...

VIVIANE: Oh? *(She takes the letter and is about to sit down at the table.)* Who on earth...

JACQUELINE *(stopping her, holding out the register)*: The postman says madame has to sign...

(VIVIANE signs and JACQUELINE leaves, upstage.)

VIVIANE *(sitting by the table)*: A registered letter... *(Opening it.)* I wonder who... *(Reading.)* "Dear Viviane..." Oh no! Not another one!... *(Continuing.)* "I'm writing for the third time to ask you to marry me..." He can't be serious!... *(Continuing.)* "I'm afraid that numbers one and two, of the twenty-sixth and twenty-seventh, may have gone astray, and I'm taking the precaution of registering number three. Please reply in care of the Hotel De Luxe, Room 124..." What kind of a joke... Whoever he is, he's not about to give up!... Well, we'll see about that!... *(Looking at the letter.)* You want a reply, my friend? All right, that's just what you'll get!... And registered, no less! *(She takes a sheet of paper, pen and ink, and begins writing.)* Direct and to the point... "Monsieur, please stop annoying me!"... There!... *(Putting the letter in an envelope, addressing it.)* "Monsieur Timothy Van Lust, Room 124, Hotel De Luxe..."

> *(She ring the bell. A moment later* JACQUELINE *appears at the door, left.)*

JACQUELINE: Madame?

VIVIANE *(giving her the letter)*: Take this letter to the post office, will you...

JACQUELINE: Very good, madame... Then what?

VIVIANE: "Then what?"... Then come back! What do you think?

JACQUELINE: Madame doesn't want me to send the letter first?

VIVIANE: Of course I do! Take it to the post office, and send it!... Then come back!

JACQUELINE: Oh...

VIVIANE: And be sure to tell the man you want to register it, Jacqueline.

JACQUELINE: Yes, madame... Before or after?

VIVIANE: Before or after what?

JACQUELINE: Before or after I send it, madame?

VIVIANE: Before, of course!... *(Aside.)* Idiot! *(To* JACQUELINE, *slowly.)* You take it to the post office, then you register it, and then you send it...

JACQUELINE: Oh... *(Nodding.)* And then I come back... I see... *(Mumbling to herself.)* Take it to the post office... Register it... Send it...

> *(She exits, upstage, and closes the door behind her.)*

VIVIANE *(brandishing the registered letter)*: Timothy Van Lust, indeed!... The nerve of some people! Who would ever think... An absolute stranger... A man I never met... And he has the nerve... He has the gall... *(There is a knock at the door, upstage.)* Who is it?

(The door opens and VAN LUST *appears.)*

VAN LUST *(entering)*: Only me, ma'am...

VIVIANE *(jumping up)*: Monsieur... Who on earth...

VAN LUST: The front door was open... I didn't think you'd mind...

VIVIANE: Who are you?

VAN LUST: Room 124...

VIVIANE *(sitting down again, agape)*: You!... Monsieur... Mister Van Lust...

VAN LUST: In person!

VIVIANE: Why... What in heaven's name... Just what do you want, monsieur?

VAN LUST: Your answer, ma'am... To my letters...

VIVIANE: My...

VAN LUST: All three of them...

VIVIANE *(recovering her aplomb)*: Yes... Well... *(Archly.)* You have it, monsieur!

VAN LUST *(puzzled)*: I do?

VIVIANE: Or at least you will shortly! The postman will be delivering it rather soon, I daresay!

VAN LUST *(overjoyed)*: The postman... You mean, you answered... Then what am I doing here?...

VIVIANE *(aside)*: Indeed!

VAN LUST *(excited)*: I should be in my room... I should be there to get it... Oh my! You'll excuse me, ma'am if I run out like this... I know it's not polite, but... Your answer, after all... I'm sorry...

(He moves upstage, as if to leave.)

VIVIANE *(getting up, calling him back)*: Monsieur... Just a moment...

VAN LUST *(at the door)*: Ma'am?

VIVIANE: Before you go... Would you mind terribly explaining... I'm really rather curious...

VAN LUST *(ingenuously)*: What about?

VIVIANE: About your... your proposal, monsieur. I believe you asked me to marry you.

VAN LUST: That's right! Three times...

VIVIANE: Quite... But you see, I'm a trifle confused. I don't recall meeting you.

VAN LUST: Oh? Don't let that bother you, ma'am! You never have!

VIVIANE: No... I didn't think so...

VAN LUST: No, no... Never... Or you'd remember!

VIVIANE: Yes... But you've seen me somewhere... That's it, isn't it?... The theater? The races?

VAN LUST: Wrong again!

VIVIANE: I beg your—

VAN LUST: Never! This is the first time I've had the pleasure...

VIVIANE *(recoiling)*: It is? *(Aside.)* Good God! Gaston was right! He must be mad! *(To* VAN LUST.*)* You mean... Never, monsieur?

VAN LUST *(categorically)*: Never!

VIVIANE *(aside, anxiously)*: And I'm all alone... *(Smiling wanly, to* VAN LUST.*)* Well... That is...

VAN LUST: I suppose you must think it's a little odd, don't you?

VIVIANE: Odd?... Why no! Why should I think... *(Aside.)* Better not upset him! *(To* VAN LUST.*)* Odd, monsieur?

VAN LUST: But you'll see... When I explain...

VIVIANE: Yes...

VAN LUST: Please... *(Pointing to the chair by the table.)* Have a seat!

VIVIANE: I... I'd just as soon stand, thank you...

VAN LUST *(sitting down on the loveseat)*: No, no... Don't be polite!... Please! Sit down!

VIVIANE *(growing more anxious)*: Of course! *(Sitting down at the table.)* If you'd rather... Whatever you say...

VAN LUST: It's really not odd at all...

VIVIANE *(trying to be agreeable)*: No... No...

VAN LUST: You see, I saw you in a studio...

VIVIANE: You saw... But I thought you just told me...

VAN LUST: Your portrait, ma'am... In an artist's studio...

VIVIANE: Oh... Oh, that...

VAN LUST: And the minute I saw you... Your portrait, that is... I couldn't believe my eyes! I cried...

VIVIANE: You did?

VAN LUST: No... "Out," I mean... "Cried out"... *(Getting carried away.)* I cried: "It's Amanda!... Good Lord, it's Amanda!"

VIVIANE: A what?

VAN LUST: Miss Amanda, ma'am... The joy of my life... My angel... My wife...

VIVIANE: Oh... Miss...

VAN LUST: But late... late...

VIVIANE: Late for what?

VAN LUST: No, no... I mean, my late wife... She's dead!

VIVIANE: She's... Oh, I'm sorry... *(Aside.)* Poor thing! That must be his trouble... He's mad with grief...

VAN LUST: I got the news from America...

VIVIANE: Tsk tsk tsk!

VAN LUST: Two weeks ago...

VIVIANE *(surprised)*: Two weeks?

VAN LUST: Just...

VIVIANE: And you're already thinking about remarrying, monsieur?

VAN LUST: Right!... But let me tell you why... My Amanda... There'll never be another one like her, ma'am... Never!... Looks... Brains... Feelings... She had everything!

VIVIANE: I'm sure...

VAN LUST: But stubborn, ma'am?... Like a mule!... That's why it happened! I told her not to take the train...

VIVIANE: Oh, you mean...

VAN LUST: She was crossing a bridge... A wooden one, and... Well, they just don't build bridges in America the way they ought to!

VIVIANE: My, my...

VAN LUST: Anyway, she was huffing and puffing across the bridge...

VIVIANE: Your wife, monsieur?... Miss Amanda?

VAN LUST: No, no... The train...

VIVIANE: Oh...

VAN LUST: And all of a sudden, it just plain collapsed! One two three!... And the whole thing fell into the Rio Grande... Train and all...

VIVIANE: How dreadful! What a loss!

VAN LUST: You can say that again! But it could have been worse! At least she was insured...

VIVIANE: The train?

VAN LUST: No, no... My Amanda...

VIVIANE *(taken aback)*: Indeed!

VAN LUST: If you marry me, ma'am, I'll insure you too!

VIVIANE: Yes... You're much too kind...

VAN LUST: Well, when I got the telegram, you can just imagine! First thing I did was go buy a ball of twine...

VIVIANE: Twine?

VAN LUST: I was crazy with grief! All I could think of was hanging myself on the spot! *(He takes a ball of twine from his pocket.)* See? I always keep it with me! I'm never without it... *(Getting up.)* Oh, it wouldn't take long, believe me!... *(Looking up at the ceiling.)* A nail... A hook... *(Spotting something, pointing.)* Like that!

VIVIANE *(frightened)*: Please, monsieur!... Please! Not here!

VAN LUST *(putting the twine back in his pocket)*: Don't worry, ma'am! I've changed my mind... For now, that is... *(He sits down again.)* And all because I saw your portrait! It was like a miracle!... I took one look and I cried: "It's Amanda!... Good Lord, it's Amanda!"

VIVIANE: Yes... I know...

VAN LUST: Because really, ma'am... Like two peas in a pod! Especially the profile... *(Getting up and going over to her.)* Excuse me... Do you mind?

(He turns her head to one side.)

VIVIANE *(resisting)*: Monsieur...

VAN LUST *(trying again)*: Please!... How else can I see what your profile looks like?

VIVIANE: But...

VAN LUST *(growing more excited)*: I have to... Don't you understand? I have to...

VIVIANE *(frightened)*: Of course, monsieur... Anything you say!... No need to get upset... *(Turning her head.)* There! I hope that's satisfactory!

VAN LUST *(staring)*: Oh, good Lord! It's... It's... *(Taking out his handkerchief, beginning to sob.)* It's...

VIVIANE *(turning to him)*: Monsieur...

VAN LUST: No, no! Don't move!

(He turns her head back to one side.)

VIVIANE: Oh!

VAN LUST: Just like that!... Please! Don't move!...

VIVIANE: But...

VAN LUST: Let me look at you...

(He sighs, sobbing.)

VIVIANE *(turning to him)*: But monsieur...

VAN LUST *(turning her head back)*: Please!...

(He continues to sob.)

VIVIANE *(aside)*: Good heavens! I can't sit here all day just to let him cry his eyes out!... *(Feeling her neck, still aside.)* Especially like this! I'm getting a stiff neck...

VAN LUST *(reaching into his pocket, very emotionally)*: Here... Let me show you her picture... You'll see...

VIVIANE *(head still turned)*: Yes, do! By all means...

VAN LUST *(handing it to her)*: You'll see! It's unbelievable...

VIVIANE *(examining it, aside)*: My goodness! Her nose... It's all crooked...

VAN LUST: You see?

VIVIANE *(handing it back, turning to him)*: Yes...

VAN LUST *(turning her head back)*: Please...

VIVIANE: Very nice, I'm sure... But don't you think... The nose, I mean...

VAN LUST: Yes, you're right... Hers is prettier... But still... You have to admit, you really could be twins!

VIVIANE *(wryly)*: Yes... Two peas in a pod!

VAN LUST: And when you look that much like someone... Well, it's just natural to expect that you should have some of their qualities... Don't you think?

VIVIANE: No doubt!

VAN LUST: Not all of them, of course! And not always the best ones...

VIVIANE: No... *(Aside.)* Mad or not, he's insufferable!

VAN LUST: Because... No offense, ma'am, but... Between you and my Amanda... Well, you know what I mean... I'm sure you wouldn't dream of suggesting...

VIVIANE *(sarcastically, turning to him)*: Heavens, no, monsieur! Why, the thought never entered my mind!

VAN LUST: My Amanda was so sweet... so simple... *(Turning her head back to the side.)* Please...

VIVIANE *(aside)*: Oh!

VAN LUST: And modest, ma'am... Modest...

VIVIANE: I'm sure!

VAN LUST: And talented! You can't imagine... Why, she spoke four languages...

VIVIANE *(aside)*: All at once, I suppose!

VAN LUST: And a musician, ma'am... She was a musician...

VIVIANE: How nice...

VAN LUST: She sang... She even composed... Ah! What a voice!... Ballads, mostly... Maybe you've heard some of them... I'll sing you my favorite...

VIVIANE *(aside)*: Oh no...

VAN LUST: We were sitting there one day... Just the two of us... And all of a sudden she opened her mouth... that sweet little mouth... and it just came out. I don't remember the words, but I'll never forget the tune... "La la la..."

(He sings his "la la la" to the tune of "Frère Jacques," with exaggerated lyricism.)

VIVIANE *(aside)*: Indeed!

VAN LUST *(waiting for a reaction)*: Well? What do you think of it?

VIVIANE: Oh, charming!... And so original!

VAN LUST *(in a sudden outburst, apostrophising)*: Ah! Amanda... Amanda... *(Beginning to sob.)* There'll never be another one like you... Never!... *(Without any transition, he throws himself at* VIVIANE's *feet.)* Please, say you'll marry me!

VIVIANE *(recoiling)*: Monsieur!

VAN LUST: You'll see... I'll make you happy! *(Grasping the legs of her chair, virtually trapping her.)* I will!... You'll see! I will!... *(Growing more and more excited.)* You believe me, don't you? You... You do think I'll make you happy?

VIVIANE: Yes... I'm sure... *(Aside.)* Good God!

VAN LUST: You'll have everything... Anything your heart desires... Anything in your wildest dreams... Nothing will be too good for you... Nothing!

VIVIANE: Really, I...

VAN LUST: You can spend all the money you want... I'm rich! It doesn't matter!... You can throw it away! You can burn it! You can... *(Reaching up and turning* VIVIANE's *head to one side.)* Please...

VIVIANE: Monsieur! How much longer...

VAN LUST: That's all I ask! Marry me, and the world is yours... As long as you show me your profile now and then...

VIVIANE: "Now and then"?... All day, you mean!

(The door, left, opens and JACQUELINE *appears.)*

JACQUELINE: Madame... *(Noticing* VAN LUST *at her feet.)* Oh, excuse me! I didn't know madame was busy! *(*VAN LUST *stands up.)* I'll tell the lady...

VIVIANE *(getting up)*: What lady, Jacqueline?

JACQUELINE: The one from madame's charity... *(Pointing down left.)* She's waiting in there.

VIVIANE *(aside)*: Thank heavens! *(To* VAN LUST.) Please excuse me, monsieur...

(She begins to leave.)

VAN LUST *(holding her back)*: Wait!... What about your answer?

VIVIANE: My... I told you... It's on the way!... Now please...

VAN LUST: And it's a "yes," ma'am, isn't it? *(Growing excited.)* It's got to be a "yes!"... I don't know what I'll do if it isn't... I don't know...

VIVIANE *(trying to calm him)*: Monsieur...

VAN LUST *(reconsidering)*: I mean... I do know! Of course I do!... *(Taking the ball of twine from his pocket.)* There's always the twine!...

VIVIANE: Please...

VAN LUST: I can change my mind again...

VIVIANE: Really... Just go back to your hotel... It's on the way, I tell you...

VAN LUST: And it's a "yes"... It's got to be!...

VIVIANE *(to* JACQUELINE, *in a whisper)*: Get rid of him, Jacqueline... But gently... The man is a raving lunatic!

VAN LUST: I can feel it in my bones...

JACQUELINE *(aside)*: He is?

VIVIANE *(to* JACQUELINE, *in a whisper)*: And don't let him back in, whatever you do!

VAN LUST: I'm sure it's a "yes"...

VIVIANE *(to* JACQUELINE, *still whispering)*: And next time, for goodness' sake, make sure you shut the front door! *(Nodding to* VAN LUST.*)* Monsieur...

(She exits, left.)

VAN LUST *(to* JACQUELINE*)*: Aren't you, miss?

JACQUELINE: Aren't I what?

VAN LUST: Sure it's a "yes"...

JACQUELINE *(aside)*: She's right! He's crazy! *(To* VAN LUST.*)* I suppose... If monsieur says so...

(There is a brief, embarrassed silence.)

VAN LUST: Tell me, miss... Who is she?

JACQUELINE: Who's who, monsieur?... Madame?

VAN LUST: No, no... The lady... From the charity... *(Pointing down left.)* In there...

JACQUELINE: Oh... From the orphanage, monsieur... Madame is in charge of raising money for the children.

VAN LUST: Ah! Good!... That's a good sign!... My Amanda took care of orphans, too!... Little birds... But still, the thought is the same...

JACQUELINE *(aside)*: Crazy!

VAN LUST *(taking out his checkbook, writing)*: Here... Give her this... I'm sure she won't object to a little contribution... Is ten thousand enough?

JACQUELINE *(laughing incredulously)*: Ten thousand francs, monsieur?

VAN LUST *(reconsidering)*: Maybe twenty...

JACQUELINE: Why not thirty while you're at it! *(Aside.)* For all the difference it makes!

VAN LUST: You're right!... Orphans, after all... *(He finishes writing, tears out the check, and gives it to her.)* See?... Rothschild...

JACQUELINE *(aside)*: Crazy, but harmless!

(VAN LUST pockets his checkbook, then stands for a moment, staring at her.)

VAN LUST: Well I'll be... You know, you look like her too!

JACQUELINE: I do?

VAN LUST: Like my Amanda!... Let's see... Turn your head...

JACQUELINE *(obliging)*: Like this?

VAN LUST *(contemplating her profile)*: Hmm!... No... I guess not... Just an illusion... *(Turning her head back.)* Sorry...

JACQUELINE: A delusion?

VAN LUST: Listen... How would you like to come to America? *(Pointing toward the door, left.)* With the two of us, I mean... When we get married...

JACQUELINE: You and the lady from the orphanage?

VAN LUST: The lady... Are you crazy?

JACQUELINE: Me? *(Aside.)* That's a good one! He's asking me...

VAN LUST *(pointing)*: With her... Viviane...

JACQUELINE *(offhand)*: Oh, I'd love to, monsieur...

VAN LUST: As soon as we get there, I'll find you a husband. What do you say to that?

JACQUELINE: Well...

VAN LUST: In fact, now that I think of it, I've got just the perfect match.

JACQUELINE *(a little facetiously)*: I hope he's tall and blond, monsieur! I just love blonds...

VAN LUST: No... No... Red...

JACQUELINE: Oh?

VAN LUST: All over... He's an Indian!

JACQUELINE: He's a... Thank you just the same! I don't think...

VAN LUST: What's the matter? An Indian is only a white man with feathers!

JACQUELINE: Yes, well... I'll take my feathers on chickens, if you don't mind! I'd like to keep my scalp!

VAN LUST: Really, he's very nice...

JACQUELINE: I'm sure! Maybe some other time... Anyway, it's getting late, monsieur... Don't you think you should be going?

VAN LUST *(taking out his watch)*: Well, now that you mention it... Besides, I have to get back to my hotel. I want to be there the minute the letter comes. The one she sent me...

JACQUELINE *(pointing down left)*: Madame?

VAN LUST: Yes... Today...

JACQUELINE: With lots of stamps, monsieur?... And it had to be "registered," or something like that?

VAN LUST: Registered?

JACQUELINE: I know... I took it to the post office myself! A little while ago...

VAN LUST: You did?... You?

JACQUELINE: Me, monsieur!

VAN LUST: You mean, you took the letter... The one she wrote... The one that's going to make me the happiest man in the world...

JACQUELINE: Well...

VAN LUST *(ecstatically)*: You... You angel!... You... *(Taking out his checkbook again.)* Here... Let me write you a check...

JACQUELINE *(laughing)*: Oh, don't bother, monsieur! *(Aside.)* No need to waste good paper!

VAN LUST: That's nice! You're not grasping... You'll wind up in the poorhouse, but still... Very nice!

JACQUELINE *(aside)*: I'll what?

VAN LUST: Well, I'm off!... *(Striding quickly to the door, upstage.)* Bye-bye!

JACQUELINE *(nodding)*: Monsieur...

VAN LUST *(stopping)*: And remember, you don't look a thing like my Amanda!

(He dashes out.)

JACQUELINE *(shaking her head)*: Out of his mind!

(The door, left, opens and VIVIANE *appears.)*

VIVIANE *(tentatively)*: Is he gone, Jacqueline?

JACQUELINE: Yes, madame... He just left!

VIVIANE: Good!

JACQUELINE: And funny? I've never seen anything like it! *(Showing her the check.)* Look! He even wrote a check for the orphanage, madame! *(Tapping her forehead, laughing.)* Thirty thousand!

VIVIANE: Poor soul! You wonder how they let people like that out on the streets!

JACQUELINE: He tried to write me one too, but I wouldn't let him.

VIVIANE: Tsk tsk tsk!

JACQUELINE: And he wanted me to go to America with him... So he could marry me off to an Indian!

VIVIANE: No!

JACQUELINE: And he told me I looked like his Amanda, or something... And he said I should turn my head...

VIVIANE: You too?

JACQUELINE: And when I did, he told me I didn't look like his Amanda at all, and he called me a "delusion"...

VIVIANE: Of all things...

JACQUELINE: What's a "delusion," madame?

(The door, upstage, opens suddenly and GASTON appears.)

GASTON: Hello!

VIVIANE: Oh! Gaston...

GASTON *(entering)*: I'm back...

VIVIANE: Cousin dear...

GASTON: And I've succeeded in securing considerable pertinent information regarding your Mister Timothy Van Lust.

VIVIANE: You have? Well, how nice... Of course, I don't really need it any more.

GASTON: Oh?

VIVIANE: No... I've already met him, poor thing!... He just left.

GASTON: He... You mean... He was here?

VIVIANE: Yes... *(Shaking her head, compassionately.)* Tsk tsk tsk!... It's really a terrible shame, you know...

JACQUELINE *(echoing)*: Tsk tsk tsk!

GASTON *(aside)*: It is?

VIVIANE: You'd think his family would put him away somewhere.

GASTON *(aside)*: "Put him away..."?

VIVIANE: For his own good, I mean...

GASTON: What on earth for?

VIVIANE: Why, the poor man is insane! *(JACQUELINE nods assent.)* You should have heard him... You should have seen...

GASTON: What are you talking about? The individual in question is in complete possession of his faculties. There's no indication whatever that his cerebral or emotional functions have deteriorated to any appreciable degree...

JACQUELINE *(to* VIVIANE*)*: Does monsieur mean that he's not insane, madame?

VIVIANE *(to* JACQUELINE*)*: Yes, that's what he means! *(To* GASTON.*)* You're doing it again!

GASTON: I am?... Doing what?

VIVIANE: You and those big words!

GASTON: Oh... Sorry!... I wasn't thinking... *(Speaking carefully.)* I was telling you about your Mister Van Lust...

VIVIANE: Yes...

GASTON: It seems he's very clever... One of those self-made men... Captain of industry and soldier of fortune, rolled into one...

JACQUELINE *(aside)*: Captain?... Soldier?...

GASTON: The kind they grow in America... You know...

JACQUELINE *(aside)*: Where was his uniform, I wonder?

GASTON: And when I say "fortune"... The man is an absolute millionaire...

JACQUELINE: What?

VIVIANE *(to* GASTON*)*: You must be joking! Him?

GASTON *(to* VIVIANE*)*: My friend says he's worth more than forty million!

JACQUELINE: Francs?

VIVIANE: Forty million?

GASTON: At least!

JACQUELINE *(aside)*: And I didn't take his check!

VIVIANE: But he can't be... That's impossible! I saw him... I talked with him... He... *(Pointing to the ceiling.)* He wanted to hang himself... With a ball of twine... He's never without it...

JACQUELINE (*to* GASTON): And he wanted to marry me off to an Indian!

GASTON: That's all well and good, but... (*Beginning to forget himself.*) Notwithstanding, I assure you...

JACQUELINE (*aside, shaking her head*): Forty million...

GASTON: The facts are incontrovertible... As heretofore enunciated...

VIVIANE: Gaston!

GASTON: Oh... Oh, sorry!... I'll—

VIVIANE (*interrupting*): I know!... You'll watch yourself!

GASTON: Like a hawk!

VIVIANE: I'm sure!

JACQUELINE (*aside*): Forty...

VIVIANE (*to* GASTON): You were saying...?

GASTON: Yes... (*Speaking carefully.*) My friend gave me all the information... The police have a file on him... (*Holding up his thumb and forefinger.*) This thick... He's not just some tourist. He's... He's practically a celebrity!

JACQUELINE (*aside*): Forty million...

VIVIANE (*to* GASTON): Oh?

GASTON: Why, for a time he was even president of some little country or other... You know... Over there... Where they grow all the bananas...

VIVIANE: Him? A president?

JACQUELINE: Damnation! (*Catching herself, putting her hand to her mouth.*) Oh!... (*To* VIVIANE.) Excuse me, madame... I... (*To* GASTON.) Excuse me, monsieur...

GASTON (*ignoring her, to* VIVIANE): Tell me, what did he say?

VIVIANE (*flustered*): Well... That I looked like his Amanda... His wife... That is, she was... But she drowned in a train...

GASTON: Oh?

VIVIANE: Even though she was insured... And he wants me to marry him because I look so much like her...

JACQUELINE (*aside*): A president...

GASTON (*to* VIVIANE): And you told him...?

VIVIANE: I... Well, I... I told him very politely that my answer was in a letter, and... and if he went back to his hotel, I was sure he would find it.

GASTON: You wrote him?

VIVIANE: Yes... Just after you left.

GASTON: What did you say?

VIVIANE: What did I... My goodness! If I knew he was a president...

GASTON: What?... Tell me...

VIVIANE: Not very much... Just a few words: "Monsieur, please stop annoying me!"

GASTON: Oh my... And you expect that's going to end it?... He'll be back, I assure you!

JACQUELINE *(aside)*: Let's hope!

VIVIANE *(to GASTON)*: No! You think...

JACQUELINE *(aside)*: "Come right in, monsieur!"

GASTON *(to VIVIANE)*: Of course! A man doesn't become a millionaire... forty times over... *(Beginning to forget himself.)* without evincing certain qualities of persistence and tenacity... *(VIVIANE sighs and shakes her head.)* And he most assuredly doesn't achieve the eminence of an executive incumbency like a presidency!... Even over there!

VIVIANE *(sarcastically)*: Most assuredly!

GASTON: No... I really envision only a single feasible expedient... I think I should go confront the gentleman *in situ,* and endeavor to convince him that the alleged resemblance between his defunct spouse and yourself is fundamentally illusory... *(Catching himself, as VIVIANE stands, hands on hips, staring at him.)* Oh... Sorry, my love!... Sorry...

VIVIANE: Please! Don't stop now!... I'm almost beginning to understand you!

GASTON: I just can't help it! It's bigger than I am... *(To JACQUELINE.)* Come... You'll stand by the front door, and if he comes back, you'll keep him out!

JACQUELINE *(to GASTON)*: Oh? *(Aside.)* Don't be too sure!

GASTON *(to JACQUELINE)*: Adamantly! Obdurately! Implacably!... Understand?

JACQUELINE: Not a blessed word!

(GASTON takes her by the hand and exits with her, upstage.)

VIVIANE *(watching him go off, with a little laugh)*: He's right, poor dear! He can't help it!... Oh well, it's not so awful... *(She sits down at the table.)* And our Mister Van Lust... Did you ever... Here I was, so sure that the man was crazy, and he's only an American... I have to admit, my answer could have been... well, a little more gentle... Especially for a man with millions!... And a president!... But what's done is done! And besides, I'm sure I won't be seeing him again, no matter what Gaston says!

(The door, upstage, opens and JACQUELINE *appears.)*

JACQUELINE *(announcing)*: Monsieur... *(Correcting herself.)* Mister Timothy Van Lust!

VIVIANE *(getting up, surprised)*: What! *(To* JACQUELINE, *in a whisper.)* But monsieur just told you...

JACQUELINE *(aside)*: Forty million, after all!

*(*VAN LUST *enters and* JACQUELINE *exits.)*

VAN LUST *(waving* VIVIANE's *letter)*: How could you, ma'am?... How could you...

VIVIANE: My letter!

VAN LUST: "Monsieur, please stop annoying me!"... That's what it says!... And you told me... You let me think it was a "yes"...

(He throws the letter down on the table.)

VIVIANE *(babbling)*: I... Monsieur, I never... I...

VAN LUST: So cruel, ma'am... How can anyone so beautiful be so cruel? How could you ever write me a letter like that?... And registered, to boot!

VIVIANE: Mister Van Lust...

VAN LUST: Once sentence... Five words...

VIVIANE: I... Excuse me... I was in a hurry...

VAN LUST: And just when I was beginning to fall in love with you...

VIVIANE: What?

VAN LUST: At first I only wanted you to marry me on account of my Amanda... Because you look so much like her... But... But now...

VIVIANE: Monsieur?

VAN LUST: But now it's because you're you!

VIVIANE: That's absurd! You don't even know me!

VAN LUST: But I do! If course I do!... I know how sweet and kind you are... And charitable, and... And I know that you speak two languages...

VIVIANE: You do?

VAN LUST *(offhand)*: Amanda spoke four, but... *(He shrugs.)* And I know that you love music... And that you write songs... Ballads, mostly... Just like her...

VIVIANE: Me?

VAN LUST: And that your favorite goes like this... "La la la la..."

(He sings, exaggeratedly as before, to the tune of "Alouette.")

VIVIANE *(stopping him)*: But monsieur...

VAN LUST: You think I don't know you, ma'am. But I can tell you everything you've done for a week... Every move you've made... Every hour of every day...

VIVIANE: You... You can't be serious, monsieur! You're joking!

VAN LUST: Try me!

VIVIANE: Very well... Yesterday!

VAN LUST: Oh, yesterday's easy!... Let's see... *(Taking a little notebook from his pocket and flipping a few pages.)* Yesterday... Yes... You left the house at two thirty-five... Had yourself driven to a shop on the Rue de Rivoli, where you bought a pair of black gloves... Went visiting... First, to number forty-two Rue Saint Dominique d'Enfer, then to number thirty-three Rue de Trévise...

VIVIANE *(agape)*: I don't believe it!

VAN LUST *(still referring to his notes)*: At three thirty you delivered Christmas presents to some poor little children... And at four you stopped into a pastry shop... Chez Julien... For a pot of tea and two cream puffs...

VIVIANE: How on earth...

VAN LUST *(sadly)*: My Amanda would have had coffee and chocolate eclairs... *(Shrugging.)* But I guess I can learn to live with tea and cream puffs!

VIVIANE: Monsieur! Will you kindly tell me precisely how you—

VIVIANE *(interrupting)*: Easy!... I had you tailed...

VIVIANE *(furious)*: You had me... You didn't! You wouldn't dare!

VAN LUST *(ingenuously)*: Why not?

VIVIANE: A lady, monsieur? You... You had the audacity...

VAN LUST: After all, if we're getting married I thought I should get to know you...

VIVIANE: Oh!... So you had me spied on, to put it bluntly!

VAN LUST: Well, I couldn't very well do it myself, ma'am! Time is money! I came here on business... Big business... Very big...

VIVIANE: Yes, no doubt...

VAN LUST: Cotton... Cacao... Bananas... You wouldn't understand...

VIVIANE: And so you had some... some individual follow me! Some detective... Or the police...

VAN LUST: Police?... No! Nothing that crude! What do you take me for?

VIVIANE *(aside)*: What, indeed!

VAN LUST: My secretary, ma'am... Very discreet... And he has a way with horses...

VIVIANE: He what?

VAN LUST: So I dressed him up, bought him a cab, and put him behind the reins.

VIVIANE: You bought him a...

VAN LUST: Yes, ma'am... First I thought I might have to buy the whole company. But then I decided one would be enough... If it was always the same one... With my secretary, that is...

VIVIANE *(incredulous)*: Are you trying to tell me I've had the same driver...?

VAN LUST: Yes, ma'am... For a week...

VIVIANE: That's impossible! I would have noticed...

VAN LUST: I don't know how... He disguised himself.

VIVIANE *(outraged)*: Oh!

VAN LUST: Each morning, a different wig... Or a beard... Or a mustache...

VIVIANE: I never...

VAN LUST: And to make sure that the doorman hailed him every time, he paid him three francs an hour.

VIVIANE: You bribed my doorman?

VAN LUST: "Bribed," ma'am?... No, I wouldn't say "bribed"... We employed him... And at a loss! You only paid two francs an hour for the cab!

VIVIANE *(sarcastically)*: Oh! *(Taking her purse out of her pocket.)* Well, you must let me make up the difference!

VAN LUST: Now, now... No need to get nasty!

VIVIANE: I beg your pardon! *(Putting back the purse.)* I am not being nasty!...

VAN LUST: One thing my Amanda didn't have was a temper!

VIVIANE: I am simply appalled, monsieur, that you would have the gall... Oh! I don't know how you do things in America, believe me... But in France, I can tell you that a man who would stoop to having a lady spied on... Well, he's certainly no gentleman!

VAN LUST *(ingenuously)*: Really?... I didn't know... *(Shrugging.)* I guess you live and learn!

VIVIANE: Yes, I guess you do!

VAN LUST: Sorry...

VIVIANE *(softening)*: Especially a man with an illustrious career... A government official...

VAN LUST: What?

VIVIANE: Like a president, for instance...

VAN LUST *(surprised)*: Like a... What do you mean?

VIVIANE: No need to pretend, monsieur! I know...

(She sits down on the loveseat.)

VAN LUST: You do?

VIVIANE: Of course!

VAN LUST: Who told you?

VIVIANE: Oh, I have my sources!

VAN LUST: Spies, you mean?

VIVIANE: Hardly, monsieur!... I know all about how you were president of... of... *(With a wave of the arm.)* Over there... That country...

VAN LUST *(modestly)*: Well... Just for four days... Hardly worth talking about...

VIVIANE *(with a little laugh)*: Four days?

VAN LUST: It could have been longer if I wanted to have my whole cabinet shot... Two dozen or so... ·

VIVIANE: Oh!

VAN LUST: But Amanda didn't think I ought to...

VIVIANE: No... I should imagine...

VAN LUST: I remember... It was a Friday... And she said, in that sweet little voice of hers: "Don't do anything rash! Let's wait until tomorrow!"... And the next day they deposed me.

VIVIANE: No!

VAN LUST: But on Sunday I was back in office... Until Tuesday... At five o'clock... On account of the papers...

VIVIANE: The papers?

VAN LUST: The newspapers! They were against me... Every one of them! On Saturday they were all for me, but on Tuesday they were yelling about corruption, or something...

VIVIANE: Tsk tsk tsk!

VAN LUST: Anyway, when I saw that, I looked at Amanda, and I told her: "Let's skedaddle!"

VIVIANE (quizzically): Monsieur?

VAN LUST: "Skedaddle"... It's an American word... It means "vamoose!"

VIVIANE: Aha...

VAN LUST: So I turned in my resignation, and we took the first boat out!... And that was the end of my "illustrious career"!

VIVIANE (laughing): I must say...

VAN LUST (sitting down at the table): Well, ma'am... Now that you know the story of my life... (Waving her letter.) I hope you'll tell me this was all a mistake...

VIVIANE: Well, I...

VAN LUST: ...and that you'll be happy to be my wife!

VIVIANE: Really, monsieur... I'm afraid... You see... You seem to be convinced that I look like your Amanda...

VAN LUST: I'll say!

VIVIANE: But that's just it! I don't!... Not really! Not if you take a good look, and compare us... Why, she's so much prettier than I am... (Correcting herself.) She was, I mean...

VAN LUST (sighing): Ah...

VIVIANE: Her nose, for instance... It had such an adorable little tilt to the left...

VAN LUST: Yes...

VIVIANE: And her mouth was much more... well, majestic!

VAN LUST: Yes... Yes...

VIVIANE: And her eyes, so much less... conspicuous!... Her jaw, so much more... determined!

VAN LUST: Yes, yes... You're right...

VIVIANE: So you see...

VAN LUST: But you have to admit, the resemblance is amazing!

VIVIANE: The resem... *(She sighs, shaking her head.)* Besides, I'm afraid there's an obstacle in your path... A rather large one...

VAN LUST: Good! I'll get rid of it!

VIVIANE: I don't think so, monsieur! It's my cousin!

VAN LUST: Your what?

VIVIANE: My cousin... Monsieur Gaston de Courvalin... You see, I love him!

VAN LUST *(jumping to his feet)*: No! Don't say that!... You don't!

VIVIANE: And I'm going to be his wife...

VAN LUST: But you can't! That's impossible!

VIVIANE: He's at your hotel this very moment... To try to explain...

VAN LUST *(distraught, pacing)*: But... But... You can't mean it!... Amanda... *(Correcting himself.)* I mean, Viviane... You can't be serious!... My hopes, my dreams...

VIVIANE: I'm terribly sorry, but you do understand...

VAN LUST: So! It's a "no," after all!... Not a "yes"...

VIVIANE: No... *(Confused.)* Yes... That is...

VAN LUST: And that's definite? Nothing can make you change your mind?

VIVIANE *(gently)*: Nothing, I'm afraid...

VAN LUST *(taking the ball of twine from his pocket)*: Well, you'll only have yourself to blame!

VIVIANE *(with a start)*: Monsieur! What are you doing?

VAN LUST: Don't say I didn't warn you! *(He climbs up on the chair, looking up at the ceiling.)* I'm sure I saw a nail...

(He begins fashioning an impromptu noose.)

VIVIANE: Oh my! *(Calling.)* Jacqueline!... Jacqueline!...

(The door, left, opens and JACQUELINE *rushes in.)*

JACQUELINE: What is it, madame?

VIVIANE *(pointing to* VAN LUST*)*: Monsieur... He wants to hang himself!

JACQUELINE: Damnation! *(Catching herself.)* Oh! Excuse me...

VIVIANE: Quick! Run and get a pair of scissors!

JACQUELINE: Yes, madame!

(She runs off, left.)

VAN LUST *(still inspecting the ceiling)*: I'm sure it was here somewhere...

VIVIANE *(hurriedly crossing right, to the sewing cabinet)*: I know I must have one...

(She rummages through the drawer. In the meantime, VAN LUST keeps looking for his nail.)

VIVIANE *(finally locating it)*: Ah!...

(He tosses the noose up to the ceiling several times.)

VIVIANE *(finding a pair of sewing scissors, holding it up)*: There!...

(JACQUELINE comes running back in, upstage, carrying a pair of large pruning shears.)

JACQUELINE *(to* VIVIANE*)*: This is all I could find...

(She stands on one side of VAN LUST, and VIVIANE on the other, instruments poised.)

VAN LUST: What are you doing?

VIVIANE: We won't let you do it, monsieur! One move, and we cut the twine!

JACQUELINE: Snip snip!

VAN LUST: You can't!... That's not fair!

JACQUELINE: Snip snip!

VIVIANE *(nodding)*: Snip snip!

VAN LUST: But... I have free will! I...

(The door, upstage, opens and GASTON enters.)

GASTON: Hello! I'm back!

VIVIANE *(running up to him)*: Gaston!

GASTON: Your Mister Van Lust isn't in...

VIVIANE: I know! He's here!... *(Pointing.)* Hanging himself!

GASTON: He is?... *(Going over to* VAN LUST.*)* I say, monsieur... I do hope that your resolve isn't immutable!

VAN LUST: Beg pardon?

GASTON: Irrevocable, that is... Uncommutable... Undeflectable...

VIVIANE *(to* VAN LUST*)*: He means he hopes you'll change your mind, monsieur!

VAN LUST: Never! When my mind is made up, it's made up!

(He tosses the noose up to the ceiling several more times, still unsuccessfully.)

GASTON: Oh well... *(Holding out a telegram.)* Then I assume you have no inclination to peruse this dispatch...

VAN LUST: A telegram?... For me?

GASTON: It was delivered to your hotel.

VAN LUST *(jumping down, grabbing the telegram, anxiously)*: Don't tell me my cotton stocks are down!... Or my cacao... *(Opening it.)* Good God! I'll be ruined!... *(Reading silently for a moment, then exclaiming.)* Oh! I don't believe it!

(The following two exclamations are simultaneous.)

VIVIANE: What is it, monsieur?

GASTON: What's the matter?

VAN LUST: My Amanda... She... She... Listen!... *(Reading aloud.)* "Amanda unhurt..."

(The following three exclamations are simultaneous.)

VIVIANE: What?

GASTON: What?

JACQUELINE: What?

VAN LUST *(reading)*: "Not dead... Excuse error... Stop... Thrown into creek... Neck deep in mud... Stop... Pulled out today..."

VIVIANE: Good heavens!

VAN LUST *(reading)*: "Cleaned up good as new..."

GASTON: Prodigious!

VAN LUST *(ecstatically, kissing the telegram)*: Ah! You wonderful telegram!... I love you! I love you!... *(To* VIVIANE.*)* Sorry, ma'am, but this changes everything...

VIVIANE: Of course!

VAN LUST: I can't possibly marry you!

VIVIANE: No, I don't imagine...

VAN LUST: But if I ever do become a widower... I mean, you never know...

VIVIANE *(taking* GASTON's *hand, to* VAN LUST*)*: I'm afraid I won't be available, monsieur!

GASTON *(lovingly)*: Viviane!

VAN LUST *(looking* GASTON *over)*: Oh, don't be too sure! Here today, gone tomorrow...

GASTON *(to* VAN LUST*)*: Much obliged!

VAN LUST: Well, I'll be on my way...

VIVIANE: Oh... One moment, monsieur... *(Reaching into her pocket, taking out his check.)* Your check... I'm sure you want it back.

VAN LUST: Don't be silly! I'm no Indian giver!

JACQUELINE *(aside)*: Him and his Indians!

VIVIANE *(to* VAN LUST*)*: But monsieur... Thirty thousand...

VAN LUST: Please!... I insist...

JACQUELINE *(aside)*: I'll take it if no one wants it!

VIVIANE: But...

VAN LUST: It's for your orphans! You can't say no!

VIVIANE: Well...

VAN LUST *(turning to* JACQUELINE*)*: Oh, and here's something for you, miss...

(He hands her his twine.)

JACQUELINE: This...?

VAN LUST: It'll bring you good luck!

JACQUELINE *(aside)*: So would a check!

VIVIANE: Jacqueline, see monsieur out...

VAN LUST *(at the door, upstage, nodding to* VIVIANE *and* GASTON *in turn)*: Well... Bye-bye!... Au revoir!

(He exits, followed by JACQUELINE.*)*

GASTON: And I should be getting back to Dunkerque, I imagine...

VIVIANE *(coyly)*: Oh? Must you?... So soon?

(She sits down on the loveseat and draws him down beside her.)

GASTON: Well, not really... I suppose there are no imperious obligations that necessitate a precipitous departure on my part...

VIVIANE *(smiling, shaking her head)*: Tsk tsk tsk!

GASTON *(catching himself)*: Oh!... Sorry, my love... But...

(The following two speeches are simultaneous.)

VIVIANE: You'll watch yourself...

GASTON: I'll watch myself...

VIVIANE *(nodding, with a laugh)*: I know, cousin dear... I know... *(She picks up the book from the end table and begins reading.)*

"Now, Poet, take thy lute. Come, kiss thy muse.
Tonight the burgeoning spring is newly born..."

(GASTON *begins dozing, as the curtain slowly falls.)*

CURTAIN